DISCARD

WHIG-LOYALISM

WHIG-LOYALISM

An Aspect of Political Ideology in the American Revolutionary Era

WILLIAM ALLEN BENTON

Rutherford • Madison • Teaneck
Fairleigh Dickinson University Press

Associated University Presses, Inc.
Cranbury, New Jersey 08512

SBN: 8386–7338–4
Printed in the United States of America

PREFACE

A great debt of gratitude is owed to those persons who have facilitated the preparation of this book. I am indebted to my teachers at the University of Pennsylvania, most of all Richard S. Dunn, who read and criticized this manuscript through several drafts as a dissertation. Several friends have read parts of the manuscript and discussed it with me. My sincere thanks go to David J. Pivar, California State College at Fullerton, Lauren F. Selden, Old Dominion College, and Dragan R. Zivojinovic, University of Belgrade, Yugoslavia. They have helped in solving many points of organization and interpretation. Robert M. Calhoon, University of North Carolina, also read this manuscript. He commented upon it in detail and offered many helpful suggestions.

The author must also acknowledge the assistance of the many librarians and manuscript curators who have aided this work, particularly the staffs of the Columbia University Library, Connecticut Historical Society, Harvard College Library, Historical Society of Pennsylvania, Huntington Library, San Marino, California, Library of Congress, Maryland Historical Society, Massachusetts Historical Society, New York Historical Society, New York Public Library, Old Colony Historical Society, Taunton, Massachusetts, Virginia Historical Society, and the William L. Clements Library, University of Michigan.

My wife Suzan has been helpful at every stage in the development of this book. She has worked closely with me on literary style, to my great benefit. Her moral support and understanding greatly facilitated the completion of this study.

In writing this monograph the author has modernized quotations to the extent of expanding most standard abbreviations and contractions; superscript letters have been reduced to line. Punctuation has been partly modernized for clarity, but the original spelling of words and capitalizations have been retained.

Hillsdale, New Jersey   W.A.B.

CONTENTS

CONTENTS

Introduction: Whig-Loyalism

Why should a man encourage and support one side of a cause and then, as it gains momentum, switch his allegiance to the other side? This is a question which must be asked about many men during the course of many revolutions. It may be asked of Edward Hyde, earl of Clarendon, who began his political career as a staunch Parliamentarian and yet became, during the English Civil War, a Royalist. The question may also be asked of the Marquis de Lafayette and the Comte de Mirabeau during the course of the French Revolution. Both men were staunch suporters of the National Assembly. Lafayette was a republican, Mirabeau president of the Jacobin Club. Yet, by 1790, Mirabeau was attempting to negotiate with King Louis XVI in order to save the monarchy. Lafayette, in 1792, attempted to use an army, put under his command by the National Assembly, to restore the monarchy.

An example contemporaneous to the American Revolution is William Pitt, earl of Chatham. Pitt was strongly pro-American before 1776. In 1766 he supported the repeal of the Stamp Act and opposed the passage of the Declaratory Act (in a minority of one in the House of Lords). In 1775 he proposed the complete withdrawal of British troops from America to create a better atmosphere for negotiation and compromise. Yet, in 1778, in his last speech before the House of Lords Chatham strongly opposed a resolution urging the recognition of an independent United States of America.

Similar examples can be found in the American colonies

during the era of the Revolution. Some Americans, such as John Dickinson, were far more belligerent in the early stages of the revolutionary crisis than they were as the crisis matured in 1775–1776. Others, including some of the most vigorous Patriots in the early years of the crisis, became active Loyalists by the time of the Revolution. It is with these men that this study is concerned and about them the question must be asked: why were these men Whigs at one stage of the Revolution and Loyalists at another, when large proportions of men clung to a single affiliation throughout the period?

My interest in this group of men who, like Clarendon, Chatham, Mirabeau and Lafayette, turned against the revolution they had helped to start was awakened several years ago when I happened to read the *Diary* of William Smith, Jr., New York historian and jurist. Smith's political career seemed to run counter to everything I had read of the revolutionary era. In the 1750's he collaborated with William Livington in the production of *The Independent Reflector* and was a founder of the Whig Club in New York City. In the 1760's Smith actively opposed the Stamp Act and was an outspoken proponent of non-importation. In 1774 and 1775 he worked actively to support the Continental Congress. In all of these actions Smith behaved as a true Patriot. Yet, in 1780, William Smith, Jr., a man who had been an advisor to the Sons of Liberty and a leader of the Whig Party in New York, was appointed Chief Justice of loyalist New York.

Had William Smith been the only prominent Patriot leader to become a Loyalist, his case would be of interest only as an isolated phenomenon. But if a significant number of Patriot leaders behave in much the same fashion—active participants in the revolutionary struggle before the war, but Loyalists during it—then the period of the American Revolution must be reexamined and reinterpreted to some extent. I therefore began to examine Smith's circle of acquaintances to see if any of them behaved as he did. Two of his friends, William Samuel Johnson of Connecticut and Peter Van Schaack of New

York, were prominent Patriots who, like Smith, later became Loyalists. I then looked to see if this pattern of behavior was exhibited by Patriots with whom Smith was not acquainted and found that several leaders of the popular cause in various colonies also became Loyalists. These men included Daniel Leonard and Benjamin Church of Massachusetts, Andrew Allen of Pennsylvania, Robert Alexander and Daniel Dulany of Maryland, and William Byrd III of Virginia. I am focusing this study on these nine prominent Whig leaders who later changed their affiliation. For lack of a better designation, I have called them the Whig-Loyalists.[1]

I do not believe that by limiting this study to these nine men I have lessened the importance of an analysis of their political behavior for an understanding of the revolutionary era. In geographical terms they represent six colonies ranging from Massachusetts to Virginia. If one compares them with the nine best known Patriot heroes of the Revolution (George Washington, Thomas Jefferson, Patrick Henry, Benjamin Franklin, Robert Morris, Alexander Hamilton, Samuel Adams, John Adams and Thomas Paine) they were collectively, as of 1765, of more political importance, had more stature, and were in most respects better symbols of the colonial establishment.

The reasons for this had little to do with their relative ages. At the time of the Stamp Act only two of these eighteen individuals, Peter Van Schaack and Alexander Hamilton, had not yet attained their twentieth birthday. To be sure, the most important member of either group at the time of the Stamp Act was Benjamin Franklin, but he was sadly out of touch

---

[1] William H. Nelson, *The American Tory* (Oxford, 1961) was the first to use this term to my knowledge. In some cases however, he misused the term Whig-Loyalist. At times he designated Whig-Loyalists as Tories and out-and-out Patriots as Whig-Loyalists. For example, he classified William Smith, Jr. with Joseph Galloway and Thomas Hutchinson as Tories (page 3 *passim*). On the other hand, he classified Edward Rutledge and Joseph Hewes, signers of the Declaration of Independence, and John Rutledge, President of South Carolina, 1776–1778, Governor, 1779–1782, as Whig-Loyalists because they were "vigorously opposed to independence." (page 132)

with colonial opinion. Daniel Dulany, William Smith and William Samuel Johnson collectively had greater influence than
any three Patriot leaders, although Patrick Henry's contribution to the opposition of the Stamp Act cannot be denied.
Daniel Leonard, Benjamin Church and John Adams were all
actively opposed to the measure in Massachusetts. William
Byrd III had been George Washington's commanding officer
during the French and Indian War and was more solidly
established in the Virginia aristocracy than was Washington.

Compared with the Tory leaders Thomas Hutchinson and
Joseph Galloway however, the Whig-Loyalists had less stature
in 1765; but Hutchinson and Galloway were isolated figures.
In fact, it is difficult to name nine really prominent Tories
in the year 1765. Besides Hutchinson and Galloway one can
mention perhaps the DeLancey family of New York, although
no single member of the family was particularly prominent
at the time. Jared Ingersoll of Connecticut and Peter Oliver
of Massachusetts are two other Stamp Act Tories who come to
mind, but neither of these men retained prominence as the
years passed and the crisis matured.

The Whig-Loyalists functioned as Patriots before the American Revolution and then became supporters of British rule in
America. Seemingly, they changed sides, broke with their old
allegiance, and joined the very faction and power they had
been fighting. The key to the understanding of these men is
the fact that they were members of the upper and upper
middle classes of colonial society. They were oligarchs and
functioned as they did for logical reasons. The Whig-Loyalists adhered to conservative Whig principles—principles which
upheld oligarchy. Therefore, their behavior can only be un-
derstood if one accepts the existence of an oligarchical pattern in American colonial politics.[2]

---

[2] On the existence of oligarchies in the colonies see: Robert R. Palmer,
The Age of the Democratic Revolution (2 vols., Princeton, 1959–1964),
I, 48–51, 185–197; Jack P. Greene, *The Quest for Power: The Lower
Houses of Assembly in the Southern Royal Colonies 1689–1776* (Chapel
Hill, 1963), 24–25.

The American Revolution was more than a war for independence and more than a civil war between two conflicting political ideologies—Whiggery and Toryism. It was also a struggle between two oligarchies in each of the colonies. By and large the colonial governments were controlled by an oligarchy consisting of the upper social and economic class. Almost all of the political leaders of the revolutionary period were members of an oligarchy in their respective colonies. Whether they were Patriots or Tories they had that in common. The Whig and Tory oligarchies were essentially identical in their functions, behavior and makeup. Composed of the social and economic elite of the colonies, these groups made policy and provided continuity for their respective political movements. Both attempted to seize and hold the reins of government in order to perpetuate the power of the oligarchy. However, the bases of their power did differ. To some extent the Whig oligarchs supported and worked through the colonial assemblies. They attempted to gain power and perpetuate their own rule by making the assembly the center of power and patronage in the colony, with themselves functioning as the leaders of the legislature.[3] Since the power of the Whig oligarchy was centered in the assembly it had some degree of popular support. This support was necessary to the existence of the oligarchy since the so-called mechanic and small farmer in America did possess important political rights. But that is not to say that politics in the American colonies were in any sense egalitarian. Although dependent upon the support of the common man, the Whig oligarchy was safeguarded by property qualifications for the participation in government and by the overrepresentation of the eastern, more settled sections of the colony.[4]

---

[3] For a fuller development of this theme see: Greene, *Quest for Power*, 11 ff.

[4] Merrill Jensen, *The Articles of Confederation: An Interpretation of the Social-Constitutional History of the American Revolution 1774–1781* (Madison, Wisconsin, 1940), 6–8. For a counterview see: Robert E. Brown, *Middle Class Democracy and the Revolution in Massachusetts,*

The oligarchies which were later to be stigmatized with the epithet "Tory" attempted to maintain a position of power by controlling the governorship and the council, although council control was contested by the Whigs in many colonies. In most respects the Tories were distrustful of representative institutions and tried to maintain their power by keeping the reins of power and patronage in the hands of the royal governor. They then hoped to be able to control this instrument of royal authority in the colonies. This stand, of necessity, meant that during the revolutionary era they supported the efforts of Parliament to centralize authority in the empire and opposed all conceptions of legislative privilege for the colonial assemblies.

It is understandable that, in some respects, historians have tended to portray the American Revolution as an intense struggle between two neatly defined parties, the Whigs and the Tories. This tidy picture of a struggle between two ideologies tends to simplify any study of the period. But in order to undertake an objective study of the Whig-Loyalists, one must reject this polarization and all sharply defined patterns of mass behavior. For the Whig-Loyalist, in essence, did not conform to the ideological pattern of either the Whig or Tory grouping.

While the Revolution did not pit neatly polarized groups of Whigs and Tories against each other, the Whig-Loyalists were not the only group to behave in what appeared to be an ambivalent fashion during these critical years. Indecision and ambivalence were important and complex factors during the revolutionary era. Several kinds of ambivalence and indecision existed in between the normal polarities of Whig and Tory, of which Whig-Loyalism is only one, albeit an extremely important one. Besides Whig-Loyalism, at least six other categories of belief and conduct that fall between the extremes of Whiggery and Toryism can be described. Firstly,

1691–1780 (Ithaca, New York, 1955) and Robert E. and B. Katherine Brown, *Virginia, 1705–1786: Democracy or Aristocracy?* (East Lansing, Michigan, 1964).

there were religious neutrals, such as Moses Brown of Providence and other Quakers, who supported the Whig cause but who could not participate in the War for Independence. They were, therefore, neither active Patriots nor Loyalists. Secondly, there were men such as Rev. William Smith, provost of the College of Philadelphia, who cautiously endorsed colonial resistance, then opposed it, but did not become an overt Loyalist. Third, there was a whole category of clergymen described by Alan Heimert as rationalists. These men were alienated from the Revolution by its Calvinist leadership and were either reluctant Patriots, outright Loyalists, or covert opponents of the Revolution.[5] Fourth, there were men such as Governor William Franklin of New Jersey and Lieutenant Governor William Bull of South Carolina, American-born crown officials who sympathized to some degree with Whig principles but nonetheless remained loyal to Great Britain. Fifth, there were neutralists like Robert Beverley of Virginia who mildly supported the Whig position during the Stamp Act crisis. They later became disenchanted with the revolutionary movement and were able to remain neutralists during the war. And last, there were men who did not openly support colonial resistance but privately sympathized with it and later became Loyalists. These men were, in effect, passive Whig-Loyalists.

Substantial differences exist between these six categories of ambivalence and the Whig-Loyalists. While these six groups of men were irresolute, the Whig-Loyalists were neither ambivalent nor indecisive. During the course of the revolutionary struggle they made decisive changes of affiliation in keeping with their ideological beliefs. During the early years of the struggle for colonial rights the Whig-Loyalists upheld the prevailing colonial notions of legislative independence. They were active Patriots during the agitation over the Stamp Act and resisted the Tory effort to centralize the empire. When

[5] Alan Heimert, *Religion and the American Mind from the Great Awakening to the Revolution* (Cambridge, Massachusetts, 1966), 413 *passim.*

open revolt began in April, 1775 the Whig-Loyalists in most cases advocated the use of armed force to gain autonomy for the colonies. But when forced to decide upon the question of independence, their fear of social upheaval and their devotion to conservative Whiggery kept all of them loyal to the empire.

The Whig-Loyalists did not become Tories in 1776. They continued to distinguish themselves from the Tories during and after the war. Thus they did not conform to the ideological pattern of either Whigs or Tories. By studying the Whig-Loyalists, one can see the danger of polarizing all Americans in the revolutionary era into two neat groups. One can also better understand the large element of conservatism in the philosophy of the American Whigs, as well as the strength of American attachment to the British empire.

WHIG-LOYALISM

1

THE WHIG-LOYALISTS

In this study the political careers and ideologies of the nine best known and most prominent Whig-Loyalists will be treated in some detail. These nine men form a manageable though somewhat elusive group. To trace the ideological development of most American leaders in the 1760's and 1770's—even of such prominent figures as George Washington—is difficult. In most cases the necessary data does not survive for pinpointing changes from mild Whig to strong Patriot, from moderate Tory to staunch Tory, or *vice versa*. Nor is it easy to trace the development in ideology by which a Whig became a Loyalist.

There exists however sufficient data to present William Byrd III, Robert Alexander, Daniel Dulany, Andrew Allen, William Smith, Peter Van Schaack, William Samuel Johnson, Daniel Leonard and Benjamin Church as a group. These men were not the only Whig-Loyalists. Other men who were Whigs at the time of the Stamp Act and throughout the pre-revolutionary struggles also became Loyalists. But there is not enough information available to enable one to trace the political development of such men as Francis Clayton of North Carolina or John Goodrich of Virginia, among others, in any detail.[1]

---

[1] Lorenzo Sabine, *Biographical Sketches of Loyalists of the American Revolution* (2 vols., Boston, 1864), I, 318, 480.

They seem to have behaved in much the same fashion as the
Whig-Loyalists under discussion here.

William Smith, Jr. (1728–1793) and Peter Van Schaack
(1747–1832) of New York are the two outstanding examples
of Whig-Loyalism. Smith was born in New York City on June
18, 1728, the eldest of fifteen children. His family was strongly
Presbyterian-Huguenot. His father was an outstanding lawyer
and had defended John Peter Zenger in 1736, but the younger
Smith was destined to outshine him. A member of the Yale
class of 1745, William Smith, Jr. later studied law under his
father with William Livingston who became his legal partner
and ultimately governor of post-revolutionary New Jersey.
In 1752 Smith consolidated his alliance with the Livingston
family by marrying his partner's cousin, Janet Livingston.
Livingston and Smith were considered to be two of the most
promising young lawyers in the colony and in 1752, at the request of the New York Assembly, prepared and published a
digest of the laws of New York.[2]

William Smith, Jr. as a person can be somewhat of an enigma.
The man that emerges from a reading of his diary is a warm
person with a quiet if somewhat sardonic sense of humor.
Yet to his enemies he appeared to be cold and conceited. He
was a staunch Presbyterian, but he had an innate sense of fair-
ness, moderation and objectivity which permitted him to be
an advocate of complete religious toleration. Smith's objectivity also allowed him to sympathize with his political opponents
and to be a fairly impartial adviser to the Royal Governors
of New York. General Robert Monckton, Sir Henry Moore,
the earl of Dunmore and William Tryon all listened to William
Smith with respect and heeded his advice.

Yet William Smith was also capable of intense partisanship
in internal New York politics and developed a fierce hatred
of his political enemies. For instance, he considered Lieutenant Governor James DeLancey to be a "demagogue" and

---

[2] *Laws of New York from the Year 1691 to 1751, Inclusive* (New York,
1752).

treated DeLancey's allies in the Council as "Knaves or Fools or both."[3] But his most intense hatred was reserved for Cadwallader Colden who succeeded DeLancey as lieutenant governor in 1762. Smith viciously characterized Colden as follows: "The Folly of his Hopes can be surpassed only by his own Wickedness & Avarice."[4] Part of William Smith's hatred of the DeLanceys and Colden can be laid to the fact that Smith was the only member of the New York Council who was not allied with the DeLanceys. "It was not a Secret," he wrote, "that I was disposed to pull down that Dominion, which the DeLancey Family had assumed & exercised in the Council."[5]

Smith's opinion of the DeLancey faction was fully reciprocated. Not content with halfway measures, William Smith was a man who employed all the tools in his possession. This caused one of his numerous political enemies to conclude that Smith was "a factious republican—a hater of monarchy—an enemy of Episcopacy, a leveller in principle, and a sly, arch, hypocritical ringleader of sedition." He nicknamed Smith "Patriotic Billy."[6] Lieutenant Governor Colden held a similar view of the only Presbyterian member of the Governor's Council. Smith was a man with "an easiness of Principles that allows him to affirm, deny or Pervert any thing," wrote Colden.[7] Yet his enemies always conceded that William Smith, Jr. was one of the finest attorneys in the colony, and Colden deplored the fact that Smith's talents were "wasted" in the Whig cause.[8]

---

[3] Diary entries, March 27, 1773; June 14, 1774; William Smith, Jr., *Historical Memoirs from 16 March 1763 to 9 July 1776* (ed. William H. W. Sabine; New York, 1956), 148, 188. Hereafter cited as *WS Diary* I.

[4] Diary entry, April 1, 1775; *ibid.*, 217.

[5] Diary entry, March 9, 1774; *ibid.*, 172.

[6] Thomas Jones, *History of New York during the Revolutionary War* (ed. Edward Floyd DeLancey; 2 vols., New York, 1879), I, 30, 41.

[7] Cadwallader Colden to Arthur Mairs, March 9, 1771; *The Colden Letter Books 1760–1775, Collections* of the New York Historical Society (2 vols., New York, 1877–1878), II, 316.

[8] Cadwallader Colden to Lord Mansfield, January 22, 1768; *ibid.*, II, 150.

Smith added another facet to his career when, in 1757, he published a history of New York.[9]

If his enemies found him to be a thorn in their sides, then his friends found William Smith to be a gentleman in every sense of the word. John Adams visited New York City in August, 1774 and was much impressed with William Smith whom he was meeting for the first time. Adams knew of Smith by reputation as "a consistent, unshaken friend to his country and her liberties. . . . [In the Stamp Act crisis] he acted an intrepid, an honest, and a prudent part." When he was introduced to Smith, Adams found him to be "a gentleman a little turned of forty, a plain composed man, to appearance," and he was highly impressed by Smith's industry. Writing about Smith and his political partners, Adams stated: "[John Morin] Scott and [William] Livingston are said to be lazy; Smith improves every moment of his time."[10] For William Smith, Jr. was not only a lawyer, politician and historian; he was interested in every facet of colonial life and was always a loving father to his ten children (only four of whom survived his own death in 1793.)

In 1763 Governor Monckton offered William Smith, Jr., then thirty-five years old, the chief justiceship of the New York Supreme Court on which his father sat as third judge. The younger Smith was a well liked and trusted adviser to the governor. The Council, dominated by Colden and the De-Lanceys, had nominated Daniel Horsmanden for the position. But Monckton resented their intrusion and because of previous affronts which Colden had shown, the governor was willing to appoint William Smith, Jr. At first Smith was inclined to accept the position which "does me so much Honour. I am con-

---

[9] *History of the Province of New-York, from the First Discovery to the Year MDCCXXXII* (London, 1757); later reprinted as volume I of *The History of the Late Province of New-York from its Discovery to the Appointment of Governor Colden, in 1762* (2 vols., New York, 1829).

[10] Diary entries, August 21, 22, 25, 1774; John Adams, *The Works of John Adams, second president of the United States* (ed. Charles Francis Adams; 10 vols., Boston, 1850–1856), II, 348–354.

tent."[11] Yet in the end he rejected the post. The fact that he
would be his father's superior rankled, and he feared his own
"Insufficiency." One probable and plausible reason for refusing the appointment was the fact that his acceptance of
the position would bring factional strife in the colony into the
open and possibly lead to royal interference in colonial affairs.
Commenting on his appointment Smith wrote: "My Principles
will make it an Event disagreeable to many—My Youth will
offend—jealousy will create enemies at the Bar."[12]

Prior to the Stamp Act, New York politics centered on the
contest between the royal governors and the Assembly. In
this clash can be discerned two embryonic political parties
within the colonial aristocracy, a court party and a popular
party. Each of these groups had an influential family as its
major source of strength. The controversy concerning the chartering of King's College in 1754 clearly illustrates the development of these factions. King's was to be established as an
Episcopal institution, but the dispute was not primarily theological, and only partly ecclesiastical. The primary issue was
who should charter the college—the New York Assembly or
the crown. Lieutenant Governor James DeLancey led the
movement for a royal charter, while the Livingston party—led
by William Smith, Jr., William Livingston and John Morin
Scott—supplied the opposition. This party soon became known
as the Presbyterian party, partly because of the nature of the
dispute and partly because the three leaders of the party,
known as the New York Triumvirate, were all of that persua-
sion. In 1758 they were able to win a notable victory at the
polls over the DeLancey, or Episcopalian faction. These factions, at the time of the Stamp Act, were to develop into New
York's Whig and Tory Parties.

Peter Van Schaack, a much younger man than William
Smith, Jr., was Smith's disciple through much of his early
career. He was born in Kinderhook, New York in March, 1747,

11 Diary entry, June 5, 1763; WS *Diary* I, 23.
12 Diary entry, July 20, 1763; *ibid.*

the youngest of seven children. Van Schaack's family was of
Dutch origin; his father was a moderately well-to-do merchant. Peter seems to have entertained some notion of joining
the army as a youth and his early schooling in Latin and the
classics was an unhappy experience for the budding soldier.
In school Peter Van Schaack's ambitions were suppressed by
the "warmth of temper and unreasonable impatience" of his
teacher.[13] His father refused to consider a military career for
him although Peter's oldest brother Henry was an officer in
the New York militia and served in the French and Indian
War. Peter studied his Latin and entered King's College in
1762, at the age of sixteen, having laid aside some of his
adolescent romanticism. At King's Van Schaack met and formed
lifelong friendships with John Jay, Gouverneur Morris and
Robert R. Livingston. His relations with Jay were particularly
cordial and the correspondence between the two men, lasting
until Jay's death in 1829, reveals a degree of amiability and
cordiality which usually exists only between brothers. While
still in school, Peter Van Schaack met and fell in love with
Elizabeth, the daughter of Henry Cruger, a wealthy New York
merchant. The romantic streak in his personality again asserted
itself and, much against the wishes of the young lady's father,
they eloped and were married in the autumn of 1765. Court-
ship and marriage do not seemed to have damaged the bride-
groom's scholarship, for he then proceeded to graduate first
in his class from King's College.

In his search for a profession, Peter Van Schaack abandoned
his father and father-in-law's trade and turned to the study
of law. First he was a clerk in the Albany law office of Peter
Silvester for eighteen months, then he entered the office of
William Smith, Jr., along with his friend Robert R. Livingston.
The study of law in colonial America was extremely labo-
rious. Since everything was written by hand, including argu-

---

[13] Henry Cruger Van Schaack, *The Life of Peter Van Schaack*, (New
York, 1842), 4. This volume is made up almost entirely of Peter Van
Schaack's letters and diary.

ments on questions of law in courts, budding lawyers were forced to serve as clerks and care for the drudgery of the everyday business in the office. Van Schaack seems to have despised this non-learning routine and when, in the course of time, he acquired his own apprentices, changed the system radically.[14] However, he did well in his apprenticeship to William Smith and in January, 1769 Peter Van Schaack was licensed to practice law before the New York Supreme Court. His rise as a lawyer was rapid, partly because of his connection with Smith, and in 1773 he was appointed to collect and revise the statutes of the colony of New York. His revision covered the period from 1691 to 1773 and was published in 1774.[15]

As William Smith's disciple, through his marriage into the Cruger family, and because of his friendship with Jay, Livingston and Morris, Peter Van Schaack allied himself with the Whig oligarchy in New York. In many respects he seems to have been more of a legalist than his mentor Smith. He retained his youthful zeal, but whereas William Smith could be violently partisan at times, the younger man displayed a coolness of judgment and the ability to weigh both sides of a question before taking a stand. Smith constantly embroiled himself in most, if not all, of the partisan struggles in the colony, while Van Schaack was often a moderate attempting to compose differences. The emotional outbursts of his youth had nothing to do with politics, but came rather when the young man married against the wishes of his father-in-law and entertained a desire, common to all boys, to become a soldier.

While at Yale College, William Smith had formed a friendship that was to last for many years with William Samuel Johnson (1727–1819), son of the Angelican rector of Stratford, Connecticut and first president of King's College. The letters which William Samuel Johnson wrote to William Smith in the years from 1744 to 1750 give the historian his best insight

---

[14] Peter Van Schaack to Henry Van Schaack, January 2, 1769; *ibid.*, 9.
[15] *Ibid.*, 15.

into the character of the youthful Johnson.[16] Born in Stratford
on October 7, 1727, Johnson remained a staunch Episcopalian
all his life, even though he was identified with the Whig cause
in Connecticut through most of his political career. Johnson's
father, the Reverend Samuel Johnson, had been raised as a
Congregationalist but had converted to the Anglican faith and
had been ordained as an Anglican clergyman in England in
1722.[17] His father and Yale College were probably the two
greatest influences in young William Samuel Johnson's life.
The Rev. Dr. Johnson came from an old Puritan family and
had been educated at Yale. A firm believer in classical studies
to discipline the mind and body, he had his son William com-
mence the study of Latin before his eighth birthday. By the
time he was ten, William Samuel Johnson was on his way to
becoming a classical scholar.

As a child, William led a life little different from that of
most colonial children with educated parents of the upper
class. There was however one pronounced difference between
the adolencence of the young Johnson and his friend Smith.
The Anglican faith was established in New York; Smith was
a Presbyterian. But no stigma was attached to one's membership in the New York colonial aristocracy because of religion.
Many of the New York aristocrats were dissenters. However,
Connecticut was overwhelmingly Congregational and the Anglicans comprised only a small minority in the colony. William
Samuel could therefore not consider himself to have been
born into the "upper crust" of society. At Yale, for instance,
Johnson stood aloof from the disorder brought upon the college by the Great Awakening.[18] He stood apart from the other
students in matters other than religion, for he considered the
college to be "Degenerated" and composed of cliques to whom
"none but their own clan are exempted from the most Severe,

[16] Most of these letters may be found in the William Samuel Johnson
Papers, Connecticut Historical Society.
[17] George Cuthbert Groce, Jr., *William Samuel Johnson: A Maker of
the Constitution* (New York, 1937), 3–4.
[18] *Ibid.*, 7–8.

not to say Inhuman Censure."[19] Johnson had to work at being "accepted" by the scions of the ruling aristocracy of the colony.

Apparently he made a successful adjustment to Yale society, for in 1744 William Samuel Johnson received a Bachelor of Arts degree and won the Berkeley Scholarship, awarded to the most proficient student of classical studies at Yale.[20] In 1747 he received an earned Master of Arts degree from Yale and an honorary M.A. from Harvard. At the age of twenty the young William Samuel Johnson was considered to be a classical scholar of some distinction in Connecticut as well as a cosmopolitan gentleman. He is known to have been an amiable person with a warm and friendly disposition, not given to quarrels or arguments.

With the zeal of a convert, the Reverend Samuel Johnson wanted his son to become an Anglican missionary. But William, like Peter Van Schaack at a later date, believed himself to be "better calculated for a Soldier than either a La[w]yer or Divine."[21] Dr. Johnson was strongly opposed to this since it was obviously motivated by a romantic view of the French wars then in progress, and in the summer of 1747, after William received the degree of Master of Arts, a compromise was reached. William Samuel Johnson would become neither a soldier nor a minister; he would study the law. There were few lawyers in colonial Connecticut, and none of sufficient reputation or skill to serve as a tutor for the young man. As he did not wish to leave home, he turned to his friend William Smith, who was studying under his father at the time, for help.[22] Smith sent Johnson a set of instructions which William Smith, Sr. had drawn up for the edification of young lawyers.[23]

---

[19] William Samuel Johnson to William Smith, Jr., 1748; William Samuel Johnson Papers, Connecticut Historical Society.

[20] Groce, *William Samuel Johnson*, 10.

[21] William Samuel Johnson to William Smith, Jr., August 8, 1746; William Samuel Johnson Papers, Connecticut Historical Society.

[22] William Samuel Johnson to William Smith, Jr., September 1, 1747; *ibid.*

[23] William Smith, Jr., to William Samuel Johnson, October 30, 1747; *ibid.*

This list of books and actual courtroom experience were William Samuel Johnson's sole initiation into the practice of law. He became even more indebted to William Smith, Jr. in 1749 when Smith sent him his first client.[24]

Johnson's connection with the Livingston faction in New York was further strengthened when William Livingston's brother, Peter Van Brugh Livingston, became one of his chief clients. In addition to his legal career, Johnson was given a large estate by his father which he invested with considerable skill. He engaged in land speculation and served as a loan broker for his legal clients. In addition he engaged in mercantile activities and owned the controlling interest in the iron mining and smelting industry in Kent, Connecticut.[25]

William Samuel Johnson was popular in his home town and in 1753 he was appointed an ensign in the Stratford Militia Regiment. He was promoted often and was a lieutenant colonel by 1774. In 1761 Johnson was elected by Stratford to the Connecticut Assembly. He was to hold this position for five years and earn a colony-wide reputation. In 1766 Johnson reached the peak of his prewar success when he was elected a member of the Governor's Council and appointed the colony's London agent. He remained in England until 1771 and served his colony conscientiously in all respects. Although his father was a staunch advocate of an American bishopric, William Samuel Johnson and his friend Jonathan Trumbull, Governor of Conecticut, were opposed to such an appointment. Johnson spent part of his time in London discouraging the establishment of an American episcopate, even though the appointment of a bishop would have been a congenial one to him personally.[26]

---

[24] William Smith, Jr. to William Samuel Johnson, June, 1749; *ibid.*
[25] Groce, *William Samuel Johnson*, 42–43.
[26] William Samuel Johnson to Samuel Johnson, June 30, 1768; Bancroft Transcripts, Connecticut Papers, New York Public Library. Jonathan Trumbull to William Samuel Johnson, December 12, 1769; *The Trumbull Papers, Collections* of the Massachusetts Historical Society, 5th series, IX, 390.

Andrew Allen (1740–1825) of Pennsylvania was a member of a prominent Philadelphia family. Born in June, 1740, he was the son of William Allen, Chief Justice of Pennsylvania. Little is known of Andrew Allen's early life, but he graduated from the College of Philadelphia (later University of Pennsylvania) in 1759. The Allen family's attachment to the college dated back to its founding in 1740. William Allen was one of the wealthiest men in America. Through dealings in land, copper mines, iron furnaces, and as a rum distiller, he amassed the largest fortune in Pennsylvania. No man in America commanded more non-landed wealth than did William Allen.[27] He was one of the founders and trustees of the College of Philadelphia. Allen's gift of £75 was the largest of any of the trustees. The first classes held by the new school took place in a warehouse on Second Street loaned by William Allen for that purpose. Andrew Allen himself was later to be an unexpected benefactor to the University of Pennsylvania for, in 1785, he was forced to contribute a fine piece of land on Fifth and Walnut Streets to the school. It had been confiscated by the Commonwealth because of his activities as a Loyalist.[28] Both father and son were also trustees of the Academy of Newark (later University of Delaware.)

After graduating from college Andrew studied law for two years under the supervision of Benjamin Chew and in 1761 followed a family tradition by entering the Middle Temple in London to complete his legal education. Andrew's father had been one of the first Pennsylvanians to be sent abroad for an education, studying at Clare Hall, Cambridge and the Middle Temple. Andrew Allen was probably sent to England to mature. As his father wrote of Andrew and another son James:

I think they are honest lads, and far from being deficient

---

[27] Carl and Jessica Bridenbaugh, *Rebels and Gentlemen: Philadelphia in the Age of Franklin* (New York, 1942; pb. edn., New York, 1962), 186.

[28] Edward Potts Cheyney, *History of the University of Pennsylvania 1740–1940* (Philadelphia, 1940,), 212.

to acquire knowledge, [are] of rather more vivacity and higher spirits than their brother John, particularly Andrew whose temper seems rather too quick.[29]

Andrews father was extremely influential in provincial affairs and was appointed Chief Justice of Pennsylvania in 1750 after having served a term as a member of the Pennsylvania Assembly, Mayor of Philadelphia, and as Recorder of Pennsylvania. Allen was a Presbyterian and opposed the Quakers in the Assembly because of their pacifist views during King George's War. As the breach between the Quaker Party and the proprietary widened, the Chief Justice became the leading spokesman of the Presbyterian or Proprietary Party, although he opposed all infringement upon colonial rights by Great Britain. His son Andrew was a Whig and an upholder of American rights even while a law student. In a brief he denied the right of the Admiralty Court to try William Heysham, master of the ship *Speedwell*, for high treason after Heysham had sailed into the French port of Cape François with a cargo of provisions. Heysham was entitled to a jury trial and Allen claimed

that the Court of Admiralty cannot with Propriety oblige any persons to answer Interrogatories which may have a Tendency to criminate themselves or subject them to a Penalty.[30]

Andrew Allen returned from his studies in England and was admitted to practice before the Pennsylvania Supreme Court on April 20, 1765. He set up his office in Philadelphia. The fact that he was William Allen's son, brother-in-law to Governor John Penn (who had married his sister Ann), and

---

[29] Ruth Mosler Kistler, "William Allen, Pennsylvania Loyalist, 1704–1780", *Lehigh County Historical Society Proceedings* (1932; pp. 45–102), 98.

[30] Undated legal opinion, Logan Papers, Historical Society of Pennsylvania.

undoubtedly a fine attorney, gave him prominence in the colony. In 1769, at the age of twenty-nine, he was appointed Attorney General of Pennsylvania.

Daniel Dulany (1722–1797) and Robert Alexander (1739?–1805) were both lawyers from Maryland. Although both became Whig-Loyalists, they had very different backgrounds. Dulany was born into one of the wealthiest families in Maryland on June 28, 1722. His father was an Irish immigrant who had arrived in Maryland in 1703 as an indentured servant. He had studied at the University of Dublin and his indenture was purchased by a Maryland lawyer, Colonel George Plater, who put the Irishman to work as a law clerk. By 1709 Daniel Dulany, the elder, had been admitted to the Maryland bar and thereafter his rise was rapid. Becoming a land speculator, loan broker and iron manufacturer, he rose to prominence as one of the finest lawyers and one of the wealthiest and most influential men in the colony.[31] The elder Dulany's political fortunes kept pace with his rising wealth and at his death in 1753 he was a member of the Maryland Council, Recorder of Annapolis, Commissary General and Judge of the Court of Vice-Admiralty.[32]

The younger Daniel Dulany grew up during his father's rise to prominence, but not as a typical colonial youth. In accord with the elder Dulany's ideas on education, Daniel received his schooling in England at Eton, Cambridge and the Middle Temple. Admitted to the Maryland bar in 1747, he was considered to have the finest legal mind in America by his enemies as well as by his friends.[33] Daniel Dulany, Jr. inherited not only his father's wealth, but also his political prominence. The elder Dulany had made the family name an influential one in the proprietary colony of Maryland. Early

---

[31] Aubrey C. Land, *The Dulanys of Maryland* (Baltimore, 1955), 1–10, 100–109. Charles Albro Barker, *The Background of the Revolution in Maryland* (New Haven, 1940), 42.

[32] Land, *Dulanys of Maryland*, 214.

[33] *Ibid.*, 220.

in the 1750's the younger Dulany was elected to the Maryland Assembly by both Frederick County and Annapolis. Upon his father's death he immediately succeeded to the post of Recorder of Annapolis and in 1758 he became Commissary General as well. By that year Dulany's influence in the colony was so great that he was made a member of the Governor's Council, although, as Governor Sharpe discovered, "he is fond of being thought a Patriot Councillor & rather inclined to serve the People than the Proprietary [as] is evident to every one."[34] Despite being in some respects opposed to the proprietary and an upholder of Whig principles, Dulany was, due to family influence, appointed Secretary of Maryland in 1761, a position his father never held. He continued in the post until the Revolution.

In 1761 Dulany went to England to enroll his son at Eton. Upon his return to Maryland in 1763 he retired from his active law practice but maintained a law office, taking only a few difficult cases which required expert opinion. He considered himself to be above party and thought of himself as a neutral in the pre-revolutionary struggles with England. However, he did not retire from his political offices and used his influence to secure political patronage for other members of his family. He succeeded so well that by 1764 Governor Sharpe believed that Dulany was "of greater Importance than ever. . . . Should his Weight and Influence be by any means increased," he would become a threat to the very existence of the proprietary interests in the colony.[35]

Little is known of the early life of Robert Alexander. Even the date and place of his birth are uncertain. He was probably born in his father's red brick mansion at Friendship, near Elkton, Cecil County, Maryland in either 1739 or 1741.[36] In

---

[34] Governor Sharpe to Cecilius Calvert, May 8, 1764; *Archives of Maryland: Correspondence of Governor Horatio Sharpe. Vol. III, 1761–1771* (ed. William Hand Browne; XIV, Baltimore, 1895), 160.

[35] *Ibid.*

[36] Janet Bassett Johnson, *Robert Alexander, Maryland Loyalist,* (New York, 1942), 7.

1744 his father, William Alexander, died and his estate passed to his only son and heir, Robert. His mother assumed responsibility for raising the boy and through careful management was able to make him a wealthy land owner, but not one of the Dulany category. Upon coming of age Robert Alexander inherited over 2000 acres of improved land in various parts of Maryland.[37] By 1762, when he had read enough law to be called to the Maryland bar, he married and moved to Baltimore. Whether he went to college in the colonies or in England, studied law under an attorney or by himself, is unknown.[38] In Baltimore he established a law practice and dealt in real estate. One of the few certain facts about his early life is that he never held office under the proprietary government. He was certainly a wealthy man, but unlike the Dulany family, the Alexanders had not attained any degree of political prominence and Robert Alexander did not move in the same social circles as did the members of the Maryland aristocracy. In all but wealth he would seem to have been a fairly typical member of the Baltimore middle class.

William Byrd III (1729–1777) of Virginia was the eldest son of the famous diarist and historian of the same name. He was born at Westover on September 6, 1729. Like Andrew Allen and Daniel Dulany, Byrd was educated at the Middle Temple. He was heir to one of the largest fortunes in the colonies. But the third William Byrd was not the man his father or grandfather had been. The first William Byrd had built up a large fortune in Virginia; the second was a man of letters and a great ornament to Virginia society. William Byrd III is a forgotten member of the family for, because of his vices and poor business judgment, he dissipated the family fortune. He was an excellent judge of horseflesh and as such was an asset to sporting Virginians. He worked very hard to improve the racing blood of his stock, but he was also a reckless gambler, albeit an unlucky one, and later became an alco-

[37] *Ibid.*, 7–10.
[38] *Ibid.*

holic.[39] By 1769 he was so deeply in debt that he stood in some danger of losing his entire estate through bankruptcy.[40] All this made Byrd somewhat of a grumpy individual, but indulgent to his children. They always complained that he never answered their letters although he seems to have indulged not only his own vices, but their every whim as well.

Because of the preeminent position of the Byrd family, William Byrd III was elected to the Virginia House of Burgesses until 1755 when he followed his grandfather and father to a seat on the Governor's Council and became a justice of the General Court. As a justice he apparently misused his position in 1766 when Colonel John Chiswell of Williamsburg murdered a merchant in cold blood. Chiswell was the father-in-law of John Robinson, Speaker of the House of Burgesses. Chiswell, Robinson and Byrd were partners in a rich lead mine in the Virginia back-country. In 1758, as commander of the Virginia militia, Byrd built a fort to guard the diggings from Indian attack and named it for Chiswell. When Colonel Chiswell was arrested for murder in 1766, Byrd and two other justices, John Blair and Presley Thornton, admitted him to bail although the General Court was not in session. This favoritism and misuse of power for the benefit of a fellow member of the Tidewater aristocracy incensed Virginians. They were outraged at the conduct of the justices. Tensions relaxed only when Chiswell, who was of unstable mind, committed suicide some weeks later.[41]

The finest period of William Byrd's life came during the French and Indian War when he was colonel in command of the Second Virginia Regiment. He was considered to be a fine soldier and was popular with his men. This latter opinion

---

[39] Carl Bridenbaugh, *Myths and Realities: Societies of the Colonial South* (1952; pb. edn., New York, 1963), 22, 27.

[40] Richard Adams to Thomas Adams, July 5, 1769; *Virginia Magazine of History and Biography* V, 133.

[41] Bridenbaugh, *Myths and Realities*, 154. Carl Bridenbaugh, *Seat of Empire: The Political Role of Eighteenth-Century Williamsburg* (1950; pb. edn., Charlottesville, Virginia, 1963), 69–70.

however did not express a mutual feeling and the poor quality of the troops he commanded caused Byrd to be extremely cautious in the field. His thoughts about the troops he commanded may be illustrated by an incident which occurred in the spring of 1759. Governor Fauquier ordered Colonel Byrd to buy two shiploads of transported convicts to bring his regiment up to authorized strength. Byrd later described these men as being as good as any recruits in the field; a fact that does not say much for the caliber of the troops Byrd had to work with, or for the opinion he held of the Virginia freeholder.[42] When the Second Virginia was disbanded in 1759 Byrd was appointed to command the First Virginia Regiment by the governor upon the resignation of Colonel George Washington.[43]

Daniel Leonard (1740–1829) was a member of the family which dominated southern Massachusetts socially and politically in the middle of the eighteenth century. Daniel was born in 1740. His father was a staunch Congregationalist, an ardent Patriot, and one of the wealthiest men in the colony, having made his fortune through the ownership of several iron foundries. Daniel Leonard graduated second in his class at Harvard and settled in Taunton, Massachusetts with a lucrative law practice after marrying Anna White, daughter of the Speaker of the Massachusetts House of Representatives. In 1769 he succeeded his father-in-law as King's Attorney for Bristol County and in 1770 was elected to the House of Representatives by the citizens of Taunton. He served in this capacity until 1774 and was a good friend and ally to John Adams. In 1772 he was elected a lieutenant colonel of the Bristol County militia.

Leonard was something of a social snob, one of the "Young

[42] Richard L. Morton, *Colonial Virginia* (2 vols., Chapel Hill, 1960), II, 729.

[43] Lawrence Henry Gipson, *The British Empire Before the American Revolution* (13 vols., Caldwell, Idaho and New York, 1936–1967), VII, 293–295.

Bloods" of Massachusetts. During the years preceding the Revolution he was thought to be a dandy and enjoyed dressing in the height of fashion. In Mercy Warren's play *The Group* (1775) Leonard was satirized as a fop and a dandy by the character named Beau Trumps.[44]

Although a wealthy man and a member of a socially important family, Daniel Leonard entered a profession—the law —which was not considered to be a gentlemanly occupation in Massachusetts. It was thought of as being just one step above the position of a barber-surgeon. Not one of the men who had landed at Plymouth Rock in 1620 had been a lawyer. It was not until 1701 that an act was passed in Massachusetts recognizing the need for a regularly trained legal profession and permitted attorneys to accept fees for their services. The position of the Massachusetts attorney in society and politics, as in most of the seventeenth and eighteenth century English speaking society, had been made eminently clear to John Adams in 1755 when he applied to become John Putnam's law student. Putnam asked: "Have you any notion, Adams, what the Province at large thinks of the profession? We are hated, mistrusted—and not without reason, considering the standards of the bar until recently.[45] Yet Daniel Leonard believed that because of his family position he was a member of the social elite of the colony and became the first attorney in Massachusetts to keep a chariot, rather than ride horseback. For daring to try to live in a manner considered to be above his occupational station Leonard was jeered at in the streets. His colleagues in the General Court and before the bar felt compelled to apologize for Daniel Leonard's grandiose pretensions.

Benjamin Church, Jr. (1734–1778) completes the list of Whig-Loyalists who are being examined in this study. Al-

---

[44] Mercy Otis Warren, *The Group* (1st edn., Boston, 1775; facsimile edn., Ann Arbor, Michigan, 1953).

[45] Quoted in: Catherine Drinker Bowen, *John Adams and the American Revolution* (New York, 1949), 140.

though his family was from Boston, Benjamin was born on August 24, 1734 in Newport, Rhode Island. His father was a deacon of Mather Byles' congregation and public auctioneer for the town of Boston. Like many children of the middle class, Benjamin entered Boston Latin School at the age of eleven and then Harvard, receiving a Bachelor of Arts degree in 1754.

Unlike the other men under study, Benjamin Church did not choose the law as a career but turned instead to the study of medicine and sailed for London where he was to study for two years at the London Medical College. He became a fine physician and was devoted to public service, making a name for himself in Boston during several small pox epidemics. He was a staunch advocate of inoculation and was thanked and complimented by the Selectmen of Boston for the free inoculations he gave to the poor.

While at Harvard Benjamin Church discovered a talent for writing verse and published several poems before his graduation. His literary ability was to be put to good use during the crises which occasioned the decade before the American Revolution. He wrote several allegorical and satirical poems about current events and people which were widely read and approved by those of Whiggish tendencies, and several "Liberty Songs" which were popular with the Sons of Liberty, a group of which he was a member. In one of his best pieces, *An Address to A Provincial Bashaw . . . . By a Son of Liberty,* he characterized Governor Francis Bernard as, among other things, a "proud Villain," a "Parricide," a "poor Tyrant," and as "The infectious Follies of a tainted Sire."[46]

Needless to say, Dr. Church was a staunch Whig and an active radical. As an active member of the Sons of Liberty he was in correspondence with John Wilkes and was intimately associated with James Otis, John Hancock and the two Adamses. He was also master of the Rising Son Masonic Lodge which

---

[46] [Benjamin Church], *An Address to A Provincial Bashaw . . . By a Son of Liberty* ([Boston], 1769), 5-8.

was overwhelmingly radical in sentiment and a member of
the Long Room and North End Clubs where he, John Adams,
Samuel Adams and James Otis wrote political propaganda.

In many respects each of the nine men under discussion was a
typical member of the mid-eighteenth-century colonial aristocracy. Regardless of colony, there were certain elements
common to these men as a group. All except one of the men
was an attorney whose position in society, with the possible
exception of Peter Van Schaack, was based on inherited landed
wealth. Of the nine Patriot leaders only Thomas Jefferson
can be compared to them in this category; only George Washington and Samuel Adams inherited a comfortably high social
standing. The other Patriots were all self-made men. William
Smith, Jr., William Samuel Johnson, Daniel Leonard, William
Byrd III, Daniel Dulany and Andrew Allen began their careers with a higher social standing than most of the Patriots,
although Johnson found it necessary to overcome the stigma
of Anglicanism in Connecticut. Peter Van Schaack, Robert
Alexander and Doctor Benjamin Church can be considered
to have risen from middle class origins and were on a par with
the Patriots at the beginning of their careers. Five of the Whig-
Loyalists were members of the Governor's Council of their
colony and five of them served in the various colonial assemblies. William Samuel Johnson, Andrew Allen, Daniel Dulany
and William Byrd III served in both houses at various times
in their careers. Perhaps they were atypical of the colonial
aristocracy in that seven of the nine men graduated from college, six in the colonies and one in England, that three studied
law at the Middle Temple in London, and that one studied
medicine in England. In most cases their sources of power were
based in the first instance on family position. Yet in the case
of six of these men, the son ultimately achieved a greater
position in the ruling oligarchy than the father had attained.
The fact that these men were members of the colonial aristocracy does not explain why they became Loyalists during

the Revolution. As R. R. Palmer has pointed out: "Without the rise of such a colonial aristocracy there could have been no successful movement against England."[47] A successful revolutionary movement in America had to contain groups of people who knew and could trust each other. These groups had to have the power and influence to attract attention to their cause and to win followers from among the populace. In addition, they had to have a degree of concern for the welfare of the American colonies. These elements were present in the colonial aristocracy. From their positions of political and social leadership they could attract the followers necessary for a successful rebellion against the mother country. The revolutionary movement in America was led, in all of the colonies, by the Whig oligarchy. The future Whig-Loyalists were members of this oligarchy.

These men were not unique in the role they played in the politics of pre-revolutionary America. They were, however, the outstanding figures who conform to the Whig-Loyalist ideology. Many Americans considered themselves, and were considered, to be Patriots in the struggles with Great Britain and later came to the conclusion that independence was the wrong course for America to pursue. Such men as John Goodrich or Francis Clayton were not as vocal as the men under discussion, but their reasons for rejecting the concept of independence were probably similar to the opinions and political philosophies expressed by the Whig-Loyalists.

Until the mid-1770's the men who later became Whig-Loyalists were able to hold their own as leaders of the colonial Whig oligarchies. They began to lose their influential positions in society and politics only as the possibility of independence first became a probability and then a reality. In the succeeding chapters the political ideology of the nine representational Whig-Loyalists will be explored.

---

[47] Palmer, *Age of the Democratic Revolution*, I, 195.

2

THE STAMP ACT

Although almost all Americans denied the right of Parliament to tax the colonies, whispers of the civil war which was to sweep the American colonies were first heard in the controversy concerning the Stamp Act. This crisis is therefore a good point to begin a study of the political ideology of the revolutionary era. For the first time all of the American colonies to take part in the Revolution were involved in writing petitions and resolves protesting a policy of the British government. For the first time riots and extra-legal paramilitary organizations were prepared for a struggle with the mother country. And for the first time there existed intercolonial organizations and an intercolonial policy of coercion—the non-importation agreements. According to many historians, notably Edmund S. Morgan, the controversy over the Stamp Act crystallized revolutionary and counter-revolutionary attitudes among the American colonists. Some of the Whig-Loyalists were extremely active in this crisis. The individual and collective roles of the Whig-Loyalists in the period from 1764 to 1766 were fundamentally and essentially Whiggish. Their attitudes were similar to those of other Whigs during this period, but differ markedly from attitudes held during this period by the Tories.

In New York the agitation against the Stamp Act was di-

rected by the leaders of the Livingston faction in New York
politics—the New York Triumvirate of William Smith, Jr.,
William Livingston and John Morin Scott. These three men
organized and were to dominate the Whig Party in New York
until the outbreak of the Revolution. William Smith and William Livingston were not only partners as lawyers but were
political partners as well. In 1752 they were joined by another
young lawyer, who had studied under William Smith, Sr.,
John Morin Scott, and wrote a weekly journal, *The Independent Reflector*, devoted to opposing the administration of the
colony.[1] Their greatest fight, and the one which led to the
suppression of the journal by the colonial government, was
their opposition to the establishment of a college in New York
City controlled by the Church of England.

The Independent Reflector was founded for the express
purpose of

> vindicating the *civil and religious* RIGHTS of my Fellow-
> Creatures: From exposing the peculiar Deformity of publick
> *Vice*, and *Corruption*; and displaying the amiable Charms
> of *Liberty*, with the detestable Nature of *Slavery* and Op-
> pression.—I have the Magnanimity to attack the Enemies
> of [the] human Race, in whatever dignified Shape they
> appear, and to burst the Chains they cast over their Species;
> To assert the native inherent Rights of Mankind. . . . Vice
> and Folly ought to be attacked where-ever they are met with;
> and especially when placed in high and conspicuous Sta-
> tions. In a Word, I shall dare to attempt the Reforming
> [of] the *Abuses of my Country*, and to point out whatever
> may tend to its Prosperity and Emolument.[2]

The editors had no desire to make money from this magazine
which dealt with controversial subjects. William Livingston
was the principal author of the essays, but William Smith

---

[1] Recently reprinted as *The Independent Reflector or Weekly Essays
on Sundry Important Subjects More particularly adapted to the Province
of New-York* (ed. Milton M. Klein; Cambridge, Massachusetts, 1963.)
[2] *Ibid.*, 56–57.

wrote at least ten of them and was co-author of four others.[3] Smith as an author dealt with many problems of a social as well as of a political nature in his essays. Although he fought the establishment of an Anglican episcopacy and opposed the establishment of King's College as an Episcopal institution, he also discussed the necessity of "instituting Grammar Schools for the Instruction of Youth, preparitory to their Admission into our intended College."[4] William Smith's pen surveyed a wide field of social problems. He denounced the British practice of transporting felons to the colonies and railed against the abuses of unqualified practitioners of medicine and the law. Smith recommended that all doctors and attorneys be licensed and regulated by the province to insure qualified help to those in need of these services.

Perhaps his finest essay dealt with the problem of the liberty of the press.[5] William Smith firmly believed that the invention of the printing press was not only a "great Means of Knowledge," but also a "grand Security of civil Liberty."[6] Freedom of the press was necessary because of its natural check on arbitrary government. This was a view with which Daniel Dulany was to find himself in complete agreement in 1765. In the preface to his famous pamphlet, *Considerations on the Propriety of Imposing Taxes in the British Colonies, For the Purpose of raising a Revenue*, Dulany stated that "liberty of the press is of the most momentous Consequence." He believed that the right to publish the truth "in its genuine language of plainness and simplicity" was one of the bases of the British constitution. Without liberty of the press, according to Dulany, the British system of government would fall.[7] To William Smith, as to Daniel Dulany, one sure sign

---

[3] *Ibid.*, 446.

[4] *Ibid.*, 419–426.

[5] *Ibid.*, 336–344. This stand was in accord with his father's views. William Smith, Sr. had defended John Peter Zenger.

[6] *Ibid.*, 337.

[7] Daniel Dulany, *Considerations on the Propriety of Imposing Taxes*

of despotism was censorship. He therefore wrote that "the Prohibition of printing any Thing, not repugnant to the Prosperity of the State, is an unjustifiable and tyrannical Usurpation."[8] Smith asked freedom, not license, for the press and supported the publication of anything not opposed to the "common Good of Society." All who opposed this were "Enemies to the Common Wealth."[9] Apparently Smith did not convince those in authority, however, for *The Independent Reflector* was suppressed less than three months later. The last issue appeared on November 22, 1753. Yet it had served its purpose. As a comprehensive statement of the liberal views of the Whigs in the pre-revolutionary period it is without parallel.

More than ten years before the crisis caused by the Stamp Act Smith and Livingston were inculcating Whig principles into the inhabitants of New York. A strong advocate of John Locke's compact theory of government, Smith wrote that "Government, at best, is a Burden, tho' a necessary one." Therefore, "Let us be content with that Portion of our national Liberty, which we thought proper to retain at the original Formation of our Community, neither encroaching on the Prerogative of the civil Magistrate, nor suffering our indisputable Rights to be invaded." Smith believed that if the government attempted to limit the natural rights of its citizens they had a right to resist. When a ruler acts contrary to the law he has broken the contract and, in effect, abdicated his throne. "Hence [the citizens] are to be considered . . . in a State of Nature," and it becomes necessary to repel force with force. Through essays such as these *The Independent Reflector* helped to spread Whig principles and liberal ideas in the years

---

in the British Colonies, For the Purpose or raising a Revenue, by Act of Parliament (North America, 1765); reprinted: Bernard Bailyn (ed.), *Pamphlets of the American Revolution 1750–1776* (Cambridge, Massachusetts, 1965), 608–609.

[8] *Independent Reflector,* 340.
[9] *Ibid.,* 341.

before New Yorkers were actively opposing the power of Great Britain.[10]

Soon after the suppression of *The Independent Reflector,* Smith, Livingston and Scott founded a Whig Club in New York City. It was an active organization, holding weekly meetings at which the memories of such men as Oliver Cromwell were toasted and Lockean ideas presented. The Whig Club has often been accused of having been the precursor of the Sons of Liberty, particularly by Lieutenant Governor Cadwallader Colden of New York and Joseph Galloway of Pennsylvania.[11] There is little evidence to support the charge that the Sons of Liberty were an outgrowth of the Whig Club.[12] It can be stated however that the founders of the club were strongly opposed to the Stamp Act, and while William Livingston and John Morin Scott were the first acknowledged leaders of the group, Smith worked behind the scenes to aid the Sons of Liberty. It is certain that the triumvirate had the confidence of the city mob. In November, 1765 a meeting held at Burn's Tavern of the "freeholders, freemen and inhabitants of the city" elected a committee to draft instructions concerning the Stamp Act for the representatives of the city in the Assembly. Smith, Livingston and Scott were members of this committee. Their resolutions urged that the citizens of New York City held that no taxes could be voted except by the people to be taxed, that jury trials should be preserved,

---

[10] *Ibid.,* 288, 290, 76–77.

[11] Carl Lotus Becker, *The History of Political Parties in the Province of New York, 1760–1776* (Madison, Wisconsin, 1909; reprinted, 1960), 49.

[12] Dorothy Rita Dillon, *The New York Triumvirate. A Study of the Legal and Political Careers of William Livingston, John Morin Scott, and William Smith, Jr.* (New York, 1949), 95–96. Henry B. Dawson, *The Sons of Liberty in New York* (Poughkeepsie, New York, 1859), 105. This view is disputed by Wilbur C. Abbott, *New York in the American Revolution* (New York and London, 1929), 44, who asserts that the Triumvirate became leaders of the Sons of Liberty and "that it was an outgrowth of this group [Whig Club] which had long directed the movements of the popular party."

and that internal taxes on the colonies were illegal.[13]

The first act in the drama to be played in New York in 1765 began during the autumn of 1764. Upon hearing news of the possibility of a stamp tax William Smith "urged the City members to Excite the Lt. Govr. (Colden) to call an Assembly." Smith was hopeful that such a meeting would discuss the Sugar Act and the proposed stamp tax. It was quite natural that the Assembly should take the lead in the opposition to the fiscal policies of the Grenville administration as it was firmly controlled by the Livingston Whigs. When the Assembly met in October, 1764 it was decided that a firm stand would have to be taken with regard to the Sugar Act and the proposed stamp tax. Therefore the Assembly suggested that the ideological leaders of the Whig Party—Smith, Livingston and Scott—write petitions of protest to the home government, even though they were not members of the Assembly. The New York Triumvirate was happy to oblige. William Smith "drew up a Representation to the Commons which was sent Home to be presented." He then gave a draft of it to John Morin Scott and William Livingston; "the former drew up a Petition to the King, & the latter one to the Lords & both went Home with the other." The Assembly thought so highly of Smith's petition that it sent a copy to Boston, probably in hopes that the Massachusetts opposition would follow New York's lead.[14]

Thus the pattern of the opposition in New York to the Sugar and Stamp Acts was laid down by William Smith. The position he assumed in his petition to the House of Commons and which was followed by the other two remonstrances was the most advanced taken by any of the colonies. William Smith based his protests to the Stamp Act on economic as well as

---

[13] *The New York Gazette or, the Weekly Post-Boy*, November 28, 1765.

[14] Diary entry, Autumn, 1764; *WS Diary* I, 23–24. The petition to the House of Commons has been most recently reprinted in Edmund S. Morgan (ed.), *Prologue to Revolution: Sources and Documents on the Stamp Act Crisis, 1764–1766* (Chapel Hill, 1959), 8–14.

constitutional grounds. He felt that the tax would "soon draw out all the little silver and gold we have" and because of this, that "this single stroke has lost Great Britain the affection of all of her Colonies."[15] He also believed that if the colonies were to submit to the tax, Americans would be "absolute Slaves" to the power of the British government. Smith and Scott both believed that the situation had arisen because Great Britain and America had conflicting economic interests. They resented the Sugar Act as well as the stamp tax and wrote that if Great Britain could not allow the colonies to write their own laws and impose their own taxes, "the Connection between them ought to cease—And sooner or later it must inevitably cease, and perhaps end in the total Ruin of one or both of them."[16] The colonists did not want or desire independence. They asked only for their rights of liberty and property which were derived both from the nature of the political contract they had entered into and the British constitution. If these rights were not acknowledged by Parliament, Smith believed "that a general Civil War will light up and rage all along the Continent."[17]

The petition that William Smith wrote to the House of Commons for the New York Assembly presented a more radical argument than the Virginia House of Burgesses presented two months later in its petition to the King and Parliament. The Virginia petitions were typical of those sent by most of the colonies. In them the Burgesses stated that in the past all laws had been derived from the consent of the people. The Sugar Act and the proposed stamp act violated this tradition. Therefore, without appealing to principles of natural rights, the Burgesses asked only that "this invaluable Birthright, descended to them from their Ancestors, in which

---

[15] William Smith to Robert Monckton, May 30, 1765; *The Aspinwall Papers, Collections* of the Massachusetts Historical Society, 4th series, X, 1871, 570–571.

[16] John Morin Scott as "Freeman," *New York Gazette*, June 6, 1765.

[17] William Smith to Robert Monckton, November 8, 1765; *WS Diary* I, 30–32. Also see: "Freeman," *New York Gazette*, June 13, 1765.

they have been protected by your Royal Predecessors, will not be suffered to receive an Injury under the Reign of your Sacred Majesty."[18] The Virginia petition to the House of Commons added only that taxes ought not to be imposed without the consent of the representatives of the people of Virginia.[19] Nowhere in any of the three petitions did the Burgesses attempt to base their protests on any but economic or traditional grounds.

In contrast to the Virginia petitions was William Smith's petition to the House of Commons for the New York Assembly. Smith not only protested against the taxation measures, but used the opportunity to castigate Great Britain for her treatment of the colonies in other spheres as well; cataloging such grievances as trade regulation, the lack of trial by jury in the Courts of Vice-Admiralty, and the issue of colonial emissions of legal tender currency. The last two issues concerned Smith greatly although he devoted less than a paragraph to make his and the Assembly's protests known. The trouble with Vice-Admiralty Courts, according to Smith, was that they circumvented the Common Law and, by placing most violations of the Navigation Acts under their jurisdiction, "subject Controversies of the utmost Importance to the Decisions of the Vice-Admiralty Courts, who proceed not according [to] the old wholesom Laws of the Land, nor are [they] always filled with Judges of approved Knowledge and Integrity."[20] Smith's argument concerning legal tender currency did not touch upon tradition; here he rested his case on the grounds of expediency. Since the colony of New York, as well as the rest of the North American colonies, did not possess very much specie the issuance of paper money "which was always supported by seasonable Taxes on our Estates; the Currency of Bills being prolonged only till we were able to burn up the Quantity from Time to Time emitted." By the

18 Morgan, *Prologue to Revolution*, 14.
19 *Ibid.*, 16.
20 *Ibid.*, 13.

use of this expedient New York was able to expand her militia and economy in time of war, as during the recently concluded French and Indian War, much more readily than would have been possible without the credit facilities provided by paper currency. By making the issuance of legal tender currency illegal, Parliament was, according to Smith, impeding the colonies in time of warfare and thereby hindering the entire British war effort as well.[21]

The most radical sections of the petition were those dealing with taxation and trade regulation. William Smith did not claim that a colonial exemption from Parliamentary taxation was a traditional right that he believed the colonists ought to enjoy, although he believed this was true and that without this exemption New York would be reduced to "absolute Ruin." He rested his case on the argument that few other Americans were willing to take up, at the time, the natural rights of man. Smith claimed that "an Exemption from the Burthen of ungranted, involuntary Taxes, must be the grand Principle of every free State. Without such a Right vested in themselves, exclusive of all others, there can be no Liberty, no Happiness, no Security; it is inseparable from the very Idea of Property, for who can call that his own, which may be taken away at the Pleasure of another?And so evidently does this appear to be the natural Right of Mankind, that even conquered tributary States . . . never were reduced to so abject and forlorn a Condition, as to yield to all the Burthens which their Conquerors might at any future Time think fit to impose."[22] He went on to reject the argument on taxation that the Virginia House of Burgesses would endorse two months later and stated that the people of New York "nobly disdain the thought of claiming that Exemption as *a Privilege.* They found it on a Basis more honourable, solid and stable; they challenge it, and glory in it as their Right."[23]

[21] *Ibid.*
[22] *Ibid.,* 9–10.
[23] *Ibid.,* 10.

William Smith also went further than most Americans were willing to go in 1765 when he declared that the questions of internal taxation and trade regulation were inseparable. He stated very clearly that Parliament had the right to regulate the trade of the empire, subordinate colonial trade to that of the mother country, and carefully enunciated that any trade "in the least Degree incompatible with the Trade and Interest of *Great-Britain*" was illegal. However, again appealing to the principle of natural rights, Smith claimed that the colonies were at liberty to engage in all trade, whether within or outside the British empire, that was not inconsistant with the superiority of the trade of Great Britain. He also stated that in establishing a commercial relationship which was not detrimental to the trade of Great Britain the colonies were entitled to "an Exemption from all Duties in such a Course of Commerce." This, to William Smith, was "the most essential of all the Rights to which" the colonies were entitled.[24]

Since William Smith conceived of both an exemption from internal taxes laid without the consent of the people and freedom from import and export duties as natural rights which all mankind should enjoy, he had little difficulty in stating that there was no difference between internal and external taxation. This was a view which few Americans would adopt until 1767 when John Dickinson's *Farmer's Letters* were published. Yet William Smith was to state in 1764 that "since all Impositions, whether they be internal Taxes, or Duties paid . . . equally diminish the Estates upon which they are charged; what avails it to any People, by which of them they are impoverished? . . . The whole Wealth of a Country may be effectually drawn off, by the Exaction of Duties, as by any other Tax upon their Estates."[25]

William Smith was not only one of the most outspoken critics of the Stamp Act in the colonies, but he was also critical of many of the bases of British control over the empire. In his

[24] *Ibid.*, 11.
[25] *Ibid.*, 12.

criticism of trade and monetary regulation, and of the Vice-Admiralty Courts, he was far in advance of most other American leaders. So much so in fact, that few Americans outside of New York in 1764 and 1765 were willing to listen to Smith. The fact that he displayed a tendency towards a more radical solution to the question of colonial rights than any other leader of the opposition to the Stamp Act with the exception of Patrick Henry placed Smith in the position of a leader who has moved ahead without waiting to see if his followers were keeping up. In the next few years, because of the leadership of such men as William Smith and Patrick Henry, the American people were to recognize the merits of the natural rights argument and ultimately the radical solution to the whole problem that William Smith and John Morin Scott were to advance throughout the summer and autumn of 1765. In his criticism of the Stamp Act however William Smith was supported by the young man who was soon to become his apprentice, Peter Van Schaack. Van Schaack was later to write that the New York agitation concerning the Stamp Act "certainly was a meritorious opposition."[26]

Colonial opposition to the Stamp Act found its focal point and received its most widely read justification when Daniel Dulany of Maryland wrote some *Considerations on the Propriety of Imposing Taxes in the British Colonies, For the Purpose of raising a Revenue, by Act of Parliament.* Parlimentary theoretical justification for the passage of the Stamp Act rested on the assumption that the American colonies were "virtually" represented in Parliament, much as were the towns of Manchester and Birmingham which were not entitled to send members to Parliament. No one doubted that the people of these areas were represented. "If," as one Member of Parliament put it, "the towns of Manchester and Birmingham sending no representatives to Parliament are notwithstanding there represented, why are not the cities of Albany and Boston equally represented

---

[26] Peter Van Schaack to John Maunsell, May 7, 1775; Van Schaack, *Peter Van Schaack,* 39.

in that assembly?"[27] Daniel Dulany, a legal theorist of some repute, believed that if this argument could be refuted then the whole of the British justification for the Stamp Act would be invalid and the act itself unconstitutional. The major purpose of *Considerations* was the refutation of the Parliamentary claim that the colonies could be justly taxed because they were virtually represented in that body. As he put the question:

It is alleged that there is a *virtual* or *implied representation* of the colonies springing out of the constitution of the British government; and it must be confessed on all hands that as the representation is not actual it is virtual or it doth not exist at all, for no third kind of representation can be imagined. The colonies claim the privilege, which is common to all *British subjects,* of being taxed *only* with their own consent given by their representatives, and all the advocates for the Stamp Act admit this claim. Whether, therefore upon the whole matter the imposition of the *stamp duties* is a *proper* exercise of constitutional authority or not depends upon a a single question, whether the Commons of Great Britain are *virtually* the representatives of the commons of America or not.[28]

Dulany therefore set about proving that a difference did exist between English electors and the colonists; between English non-electors and the colonists. English electors, being on the scene, were able to make their wishes known regarding the adviseability of the passage of a new law. When a law was found to be a threat to liberty or, as Dulany stated, "productive of hardships or inconvenience" the electors could instruct their delegates to procure a repeal. "But who are the representatives of the colonies? To whom shall *They* send their instructions when desirous to obtain the repeal of a law striking at the root and foundation of every civil right...?"

[27] Soame Jenyns, *The Objections to the Taxation of Our American Colonies . . . Considered* (London, 1765), quoted in Bailyn, *Pamphlets of the American Revolution,* 601.
[28] Dulany, *Considerations,* 610.

Obviously the sending of instructions to every member of the House of Commons would be improper. In such a case the only feasible mode of communication would be by petition "in which an unreserved style would probably be deemed indecency and strong expressions insolence, in which a claim of rights may not, perhaps, be explained or even insinuated if to impugn or glance at their authority whose relief is supplicated." An obvious difference between the colonists and British electors therefore existed.[29]

But it could be claimed that while the colonists differed from British electors, they were both involved in the same legislation, in the same taxation. Therefore the colonists and the electors were linked by an "intimate and inseparable" relationship, since what affected one also affected the other, in much the same manner as English electors and non-electors were related. This, Dulany stated, was not so. In fact, just the opposite could be true. The colonists could be oppressed in many ways without exciting any sympathy or alarm in Great Britain, while any act affecting English non-electors would have an immediate effect upon electors. "Moreover, even acts oppressive and injurious to the colonies in an extreme degree might become popular in England from the promise or expectation that the very measures which depressed the colonies would give ease to the inhabitants of Great Britain." Yet Dulany was forced to admit that, since the interests of the various branches of the British empire were allied, any act adversely affecting the colonies would have an eventual effect on England. But, he added, "these consequences being generally remote are not at once forseen. They do not immediately alarm the fears and engage the passions of the English electors" since the relationship between the colonist and the Englishman was tenuous and "deductible only through a train of reasoning which few will take the trouble or can have the opportunity, if they have the capacity, to investigate." Therefore the rela-

---

[29] *Ibid.*, 608.

tionship between colonist and English elector "is a knot too
infirm to be relied on as a competent security" against the
oppression of the colonies by Parliament.[30]

Besides, there was one vital difference between English non-
electors and the colonists. The English non-elector could, upon the acquisition of the required freehold, become eligible
to vote in Parliamentary elections. But, by no stretch of the
imagination could an American hope to exercise the same
privilege; unless, of course, he moved to England. Even if
every colonists possessed the required freehold they could not
vote since the privilege of participating in elections required
that the vote be exercised in person. Since no Parliamentary
elections took place in the colonies, no colonist, no matter how
wealthy or qualified, could vote for members of Parliament.[31]
Because of these various factors Daniel Dulany was able to
prove to his own satisfaction and to the satisfaction of most
colonists and many Englishmen that the colonies were not
represented, either actually or virtually, in Parliament.

Having destroyed the theoretical basis for Parliamentary
taxation of the American colonies, Daniel Dulany proceeded
to demonstrate the unconstitutionality of the Stamp Act. The
colonists were not in any way represented in the House of
Commons. And since "the Commons of Great Britain have no
right by the constitution to GIVE AND GRANT property *not*
belonging to themselves" or those whom they represent, "then
the principle of the Stamp Act must be given up as inde-
fensible."[32]

Dulany was quick to point out however that even though
Parliament had no right to tax the colonies, the colonists could
be taxed. The author of *Considerations* stated very clearly that
one of the essential principles of the British constitution was
"that the subject shall not be taxed without his consent."[33] The

---

[30] *Ibid.*, 615.
[31] *Ibid.*, 614.
[32] *Ibid.*, 615–616.
[33] *Ibid.*, 612.

colonists elected their own representative assemblies which had "a regular, adequate, and constitutional authority to tax them." The fact that the colonists could not be taxed by Parliament because of non-representation would not by any means lead to "an iniquitous and absurd exemption" from all taxation as some of the Stamp Act's advocates assumed.[34] Rather, in claiming an exemption from Parliamentary taxation the colonists were insuring the security of the rights and property to which, Dulany believed, they were entitled by the British constitution, the colonial charters and the Common Law. It was only in the colonial assembly that the colonists exercised a share in government and exercised the same rights and privileges, with as much security, as an English elector represented in the House of Commons. "For," as Daniel Dulany believed, "the words *Parliament* and *Assembly* are in this respect only different terms to express the same thing."[35]

The fact that Dulany had found that Parliament did not possess any legitimate authority to tax the colonies did not mean however that the colonies were not subordinate to Great Britain or Parliament. Nor did the fact that the Stamp Act was unconstitutional mean that the colonists were absolved from any duty to obey it. For Daniel Dulany was a legalist and strongly opposed to any action which was in any way subversive of law and authority. Believing the Stamp Act to be unconstitutional did not mean, to Dulany, that it did not have the force of law in the colonies. Laws, whether constitutional or unconstitutional, valid or invalid, had to be obeyed if a breakdown of all authority and consequent anarchy were to be avoided. Dulany could, and did, therefore argue at the same time as he was proving the act unconstitutional and invalid that the colonists should submit to the law "whilst it endures."[36]

Considerations was written not so much to incite the people

[34] *Ibid.*, 615.
[35] *Ibid.*, 633–634.
[36] *Ibid.*, 611–612.

of America to opposition as it was to convince Englishmen that a repeal of the law was not only desirous, but obligatory under the terms of the British constitution and the Common Law. Dulany, having proved the Stamp Act unconstitutional according to Parliament's own principles, could have rested his case at that point. However he did not wish to totally destroy Parliamentary authority, but had merely set out to ascertain the proper limits of it. And so, he was very careful to assert, in the strongest terms, that the colonies were fully subordinate to Great Britain. Even while denying Parliament the right to tax the colonies, Dulany claimed that the colonies acknowledged their dependence on and subordination to England, "and that the authority vested in the supreme council of the nation may be justly exercised to support and preserve that subordination." This authority resulted from and was implicit in the existing relationship between England and her colonies. But the degree of colonial subordination did not mean that England had "a right to seize the property of his inferior when he pleases or to command him in everything since, in the degrees of it, there may very well exist a *dependence* and *inferiority* without absolute *vassalage* and *slavery*. In what the superior may *rightfully* control or compel, and in what the inferior ought to be at liberty to act without control or compulsion, depends upon the very nature of the dependence and the degree of the subordination." Dulany defined the words "dependence" and "subordination" in Lockean terms; for Daniel Dulany was a true Whig and a firm believer in the philosophy of John Locke. He believed that American rights, as expressed in the colonial charters, were "founded upon the inalienable rights of the subject and upon the most sacred compact . . . [and] upon principles on which their compact with the crown was originally founded." The Maryland lawyer stated that when the relationship between the contracting parties had been formalized by "express compact," as in the case of Great Britain and her colonies, then the superior partner was limited in its authority "by the powers vested in the inferior," as was the case with regard to the Stamp Act. Parliament therefore possessed the right to promulgate such acts as were "necessary or proper for preserving or securing the dependence of the colonies" but not those which were "not necessary or proper for that very important purpose." The dependence of the colonies was doubly assured for, although the colonial legislatures were "empowered to impose internal taxes," their legislative authority was limited and subordinated for they were "restrained from making acts of Assembly repugnant to the laws of England." Thus, to Daniel Dulany, the colonies and Great Britain lived together harmoniously in the British empire, each branch secure in its relationship with the other. The only thing which could disturb the existence of the empire was an attempt by one branch to assert its superiority over the other by unconstitutional means or for the other branch to attempt to cast off its dependency and assert its independence. It is clear that Daniel Dulany believed that the former action had taken place; it is equally clear that he hoped the latter never would.[37]

It has often been asserted that at the time of the Stamp Act the colonists created an artificial dichotomy between internally and externally imposed taxes. They are said to have stated that internal taxes such as the Stamp Act were unconstitutional, while external taxes—import and export duties—were legal.[38] To some extent this dichotomy is supported by Dulany's *Considerations,* although the author made no real distinction between internally and externally levied revenue-producing taxes. However Dulany made a clear distinction between an act, such as the Stamp Act, which imposed "a tax for *the single purpose*

---

[37] *Ibid.,* 619, 620, 632, 634. For Dulany's use of a Whig interpretation of history see: H. Trevor Colbourn, *The Lamp of Experience: Whig History and the Intellectual Origins of the American Revolution* (Chapel Hill, 1965), 135–137.

[38] Edmund S. and Helen M. Morgan, *The Stamp Act Crisis, Prologue to Revolution* (Chapel Hill, 1953), 34–39, 98, 114–115. Carl Lotus Becker, *The Declaration of Independence: A Study in the History of Political Ideas* (New York, 1922), 90.

of revenue and those acts which have been made for the regulation of trade and have produced some revenue *in consequence of their effect* and operation as *regulations of trade."* He considered an external tax to be just as unconstitutional as an internal one, but made a distinction between taxes and regulations of trade. Any sort of tax on colonial property instituted without the consent of the colonists was clearly illegal, no matter how levied. But Parliament as the supreme legislative body in the British empire did possess the right to regulate the trade of the empire. As far as Dulany was concerned, "not only the welfare but perhaps the existence of the mother country as an independent kingdom may depend upon her trade and navigation." Therefore a denial of the right to regulate the trade of the empire "would contradict the admission of the subordination and of the authority to preserve it resulting from the nature of the relation between the mother country and her colonies." This regulation commonly took the form of import and export duties which, of course, produced a revenue. Since the authority to regulate trade was "unquestionable," and an "incidental revenue" was produced as a consequence, the incidental revenue was "not therefore unwarrantable."[39]

Dulany went on to state that Great Britain had no right "to impose an internal tax on the colonies without their consent *for the single purpose of revenue."* But he admitted that Parliament had a right to regulate colonial trade. Hence it might be said that Dulany differentiated between internal and external taxes. But this was not so. To Daniel Dulany any act which had as its main purpose the production of a revenue was an internal tax no matter how it was levied. In this definition he followed the British supporters of the Stamp Act who claimed that Parliament had many times in the past levied internal taxes upon the colonies and therefore the Stamp Act was not an innovation. In effect they stated "that the duties

---

[39] Dulany, *Considerations,* 637–638.

upon any exports or imports are internal taxes." Dulany, utiliz-
ing this definition, denied Parliament the right to levy any taxes
without the content of those to be taxed. He admitted however that Parliament could regulate trade and that this might
produce an incidental revenue. But these measures were not
taxes so long as their major purpose was regulation. If an act
regulating trade was to be passed which had as its major
purpose the production of a revenue then it was a tax and
therefore unconsitutional.[40]

Daniel Dulany even took this argument one step further.
He clearly stated that trade regulations designed to restrain
the colonies "from exporting its produce to the most profitable
market *in favor of another*," or obliged them "to import the
manufactures of one country that are dear instead of those of
another that are cheap" was, in effect, a tax upon the colonies.
As he pointed out, by being forced to trade with Great Britain the colonies were being taxed for the benefit of England.
This tax was equal to the amount lost by being forced to buy
and sell in the more expensive English market. Hence, to Dulany it appeared that England gained as much in this way as
she would if trade were permitted with other nations and a
proportional tax paid to equalize the price. This conferred a
monopoly upon Great Britain and was therefore as much a
tax as the Stamp Act.[41]

Having dealt with the illegality of Parliamentary taxation
and having defined the nature of the relationship between
Great Britain and the American colonies, Daniel Dulany attempted to find a legal method by which the colonies could
protest against the unconstitutional measures. He wanted no
part of mob action or illegal methods of protest. Although
Parliament had erred in passing the Stamp Act and some of
the Navigation Acts, Americans could not compound the
error with unconstitutional means of protest. Above all else,
the Maryland lawyer was a firm believer in law and order. His

[40] *Ibid.*
[41] *Ibid.*, 652–653 ff.

proposals concerning the means of persuading Parliament to repeal the measure were therefore more moderate than his constitutional arguments. Dulany believed that the colonies were extremely fortunate in that for the necessities of life, food and clothing, the colonists were not dependent upon Great Britain. They were however dependent upon Great Britain for many luxuries, which "ought for the most part to be ranked among the comforts and decencies of life." But Dulany firmly believed that these could "be provided by domestic industry." This was the crux of Dulany's proposal. The colonies could produce all of the necessities of life through diligent application to home industry. They could thus be independent of British products, attain economic self-sufficiency, and at the same time effectively protest against the unconstitutional measures. The economy of the British Isles would soon suffer. By the means of home production "the consequence of oppression in the colonies to the inhabitants of Great Britain would strike home, and immediately. None would mistake it." Though progress might be slow in attaining the same high quality in manufactured goods, Americans would find "that practice will confer knowledge and skill." In the meantime America could take pride in its own efforts. "Let the manufacture of America be the symbol of dignity, the badge of virtue, and it will soon break the fetters of distress. A garment of linsey-woolsey, when made the distinction of real patriotism, is more honorable and attractive of respect and veneration than all the pageantry and the robes and the plumes and the diadem of an emperor without it. Let the emulation be not in the richness and variety of foreign productions, but in the improvement and perfection of our own." In this way the colonies would be united, and Britain would pay the penalty of tyranny.[42]

This argument was more radical than his ideas for effecting such a course of action. Dulany did not believe that an application to home-spun and the consequent non-importation of

---

[42] *Ibid.*, 648–650.

British goods could be put into effect by the colonial assemblies. He did not think that they possessed the legal "power to encourage by laws the prosecution of this beneficial, this necessary measure." He did however believe that the legislators "might promote it almost as effectually by their example." "The sight of our representatives, all adorned in complete dresses of their own leather and flax and wool, manufactured by the art and industry of the inhabitants of Virginia [or any other colony], would excite, not the gaze of admiration, the flutter of an agitated imagination, or the momentary amusement of a transient scene, but a calm, solid, heart-felt delight."[43] This idea, under the names of non-importation, non-intercourse and non-consumption, was to be a strong weapon in the hands of the colonists during the remainder of the pre-revolutionary struggles with Great Britain.

Daniel Dulany's arguments and ideas were not so radically oriented as were William Smith's and perhaps for that reason commanded a wider range of support. But Dulany, like Smith before him, used his pamphlet not only as a vehicle from which to attack the Stamp Act and trade regulations but also as a means of expressing his conception of American rights in a wide range of fields. Dulany did not afford the same emphasis to the natural rights argument that William Smith had advanced but did nonetheless believe that democracy "which is as much a part of the constitution as monarchy or aristocracy" had a firm place in the British system of government. Democracy could not exist if "the people are excluded from a share in the executing and a share in the making of laws" as was the case with the Navigation and Stamp Acts. But these were not the only violations of the constitution for which Dulany demanded redress. Like William Smith before him Dulany protested against the establishment of Vice-Admiralty Courts in the colonies, the consequent loss to the colonists of trial by jury, and the establishment of arbitrary law. His means of protest

---

[43] *Ibid.*, 651.

for these actions were the same as his protest to the Stamp Act—non-importation.[44] The fact that Dulany's *Considerations* appealed to most Americans and was widely read and hailed shows to some extent that most colonists were not yet ready for an appeal to natural rights or for the radical solutions to the crisis presented by such men as William Smith or Patrick Henry. At the time of the Stamp Act public opinion in the colonies was much more moderate in tone than it was to be as the era progressed and political thought matured.

On February 28, 1766 some of the citizens of Baltimore County, Maryland organized themselves into an association which they called "The Society for the Maintenance of Order and the Protection of American Liberty."[45] This group, popularly known as the Sons of Liberty, was led by Robert Alexander, William Lux and Thomas Chase. They, with the aid of D. Chamier and Robert Adair, made up the committee of correspondence of the Baltimore Sons of Liberty.[46] Alexander's role in the Stamp Act agitation marked the future Whig-Loyalist's debut on the political stage. He immediately found himself at odds with another future Whig-Loyalist, Daniel Dulany, for he was willing to "pursue every necessary method to oppose the Introduction of that [Stamp Act], or any other oppressive, arbitrary, and illegal Measure," while Dulany limited his opposition to constitutional means of protest.[47]

As Secretary of the Province of Maryland Daniel Dulany kept the records of the courts of law. One of the first acts of the Sons of Liberty was to demand that the law courts proceed with their business without the use of stamped paper. To open the courts without the use of stamps meant that Dulany would have to violate the law. This he was not willing to do, saying

---

[44] *Ibid.*, 609, 627, 629–630.

[45] John Thomas Scharf, *The Chronicles of Baltimore* (Baltimore, 1874), 58.

[46] Johnson, *Robert Alexander*, 22.

[47] Thomas Chase, William Lux, D. Chamier, Robert Alexander and Robert Adair to the New York Sons of Liberty, March 9, 1766; Lamb Papers, New York Historical Society.

that "In Proceeding to Business at this time, I should Act against my own Sentiments," and offered to resign his position rather than violate a law, albeit an illegal one.[48] As a constitutional lawyer, Daniel Dulany firmly believed that Americans should obey the Stamp Act, although it was unconstitutional, until its repeal, rather than violate the law. Alexander and the Sons of Liberty of course did not agree with this argument. However Dulany's quarrel with the Sons of Liberty died a natural death when news of the repeal of the Stamp Act reached Maryland.

Daniel Dulany had opposed the Stamp Act, but as an official of the proprietary government of Maryland did not act in accord with the Sons of Liberty. In Connecticut, however, William Samuel Johnson worked within the framework of the colonial government and with the Sons of Liberty to force the repeal of the Stamp Act.

William Samuel Johnson and his good friend Jared Ingersoll portray a study in contrasts when one considers their reactions to the issue raised by the Stamp Act. The friendship between the two men began during their student days at Yale, although Ingersoll was Johnson's senior by two years. Both became successful lawyers and their standing in the upper class of Connecticut society was similar. Although they were to remain good friends until Jared Ingersoll's death in 1781, they found themselves at odds politically in the period prior to the Declaration of Independence. Both men became Loyalists during the Revolution. However they played very different roles before the outbreak of the war. William Samuel Johnson was a Whig and a patriot. Jared Ingersoll was a Tory.

Johnson was a member of the Connecticut Assembly when news of the passage of the Stamp Act reached that colony.

---

[48] Daniel Dulany to the Council of Maryland, February 26, 1766; *Archives of Maryland: Proceedings of the Council of Maryland, April 15, 1761–September 24, 1770* (ed. William Hand Browne; XXXII, Baltimore, 1912), 122.

His initial reaction to the news was one of horror, and using his position in the Assembly, he denounced the act in ringing terms, asserting that the purpose of the Grenville ministry was to reduce the colonists to the position of "absolute slaves."[49] But then Johnson relented and for a short time was willing to submit to the authority of Parliament, since news had reached the colony that his friend Jared Ingersoll was to be the Distributor of Stamps, although he still believed that to submit was slavery. He wrote to Ingersoll saying:

> Since we are doomed to Stamps and Slavery & must submit, we hear with pleasure that your gentle hand will fit on our Chains & Shackles, who I know will make them set easie as possible .... If you propose to have a Subaltern in every town I shall be at your service for Stratford if it is agreeable.[50]

Johnson, having misjudged the temper of the people, soon repented having made this last proposal and returned to the radical fold, becoming one of the leaders of the agitation against the Stamp Act in Connecticut.

Jared Ingersoll was in England as Connecticut agent at the time when the Grenville ministry was considering the measures to be taken with regard to the taxation of the American colonies. At first he opposed Grenville's policies, but the more he studied the proposed tax measure the less he thought it an unjust one. He also came to the conclusion that an organized administration extending throughout the empire would be extremely beneficial to the American colonies. While he did not like to see additional taxes imposed on the colonies since this would place them under the direct control of Parlia-

---

[49] Groce, *William Samuel Johnson,* 55.

[50] William Samuel Johnson to Jared Ingersoll, June 3, 1765; Franklin B. Dexter (ed.), "A Selection from the Correspondence and Miscellaneous Papers of Jared Ingersoll," *Papers* of the New Haven Colony Historical Society, IX (1918), 324–325.

ment, Ingersoll believed that the advantages of unity would more than compensate for the disadvantages that the colonies would be placed under.[51] Ingersoll's friend Thomas Whately, the Secretary of the Treasury, was working on the final revision of the stamp bill and Ingersoll aided him in this task, doing all in his power to lessen the duties. As he later wrote:

> This task I was very glad to understake, as I very well knew the information I must give would operate strongly in our favour, as the number of our Law Suits, Deeds, Tavern Licenses & in short almost all the Objects of the intended taxation & Duties are so very numerous in the Colony that the knowledge of them would tend to the imposing a Duty so much the Lower as the Objects were more in Number. This Effect I flatter myself it has had in some measure. Mr. Whately to be sure tells me I may fairly claim the honour of having occasioned the Duty's being much lower than was intended.[52]

He later accepted the post of Distributor of Stamps for Connecticut, believing that "I should be able to assist you to the Construction and Application of the Act; better than a stranger not acquainted with our methods."[53]

Ingersoll was never able to accomplish these ends. Typical of the response to his appointment as Stamp Distributor were two literary efforts by Dr. Benjamin Church of Boston. These were a poem and a pamphlet. It was during the agitation over the Stamp Act that physical intimidation first played a part in the revolutionary movement. Mob violence, although never bloodshed, was to terrorize those who supported the British

---

[51] Lawrence Henry Gipson, *Jared Ingersoll: A Study of American Loyalism in Relation to British Colonial Government* (New Haven, 1920), 136–137.

[52] Jared Ingersoll to Thomas Fitch, 1765; "Ingersoll Correspondence," 306–315.

[53] Jared Ingersoll "To the Public"; *Connecticut Gazette,* September 6, 1765.

during the struggle for American rights. This was first seen in Boston on August 14, 1765 when a destructive mob hung an effigy of the Massachusetts Stamp Distributor, Andrew Oliver, from a tree. This action was politically inspired and oriented. The mob demolished the office Oliver was to use as the stamp distribution center and partially destroyed his home. The next day, having been thoroughly intimidated, Oliver resigned his distributorship. When Lieutenant Governor Thomas Hutchinson attempted to intervene to protect Oliver's property he was marked as a friend to the Stamp Act and his home was wrecked by the mob.[54]

Resistance to the Stamp Act in Connecticut followed the pattern established in Boston. When news of the act's passage reached the colony, groups began to form to oppose its implimentation. These men called themselves the Sons of Liberty. When Jared Ingersoll appeared as Distributor of Stamps the Sons of Liberty found a focal point for their attacks upon the hated measure. Taking their cut from Boston, mobs burned Ingersoll in effigy in Norwich, New London and other towns. When Ingersoll did not heed these warnings he was faced with direct intimidation and, in mid-September, was forced to resign and swear that he would never attempt to distribute stamps in Connecticut.

The burning of Ingersoll's effigy at New London was extremely elaborate. According to the newspaper accounts, the effigy was placed upon a gallows "with a boot [Lord Bute] placed a little back of his right shoulder." It was then carried through the town to the accompaniment of music, guns and the approval of the crowd. Finally the effigy was rehung and burned to the cheers of the populace and "the guns on the battery were repeatedly discharged." The burning was occasioned, according to the same account, by children shouting "THENCE HANGS A TRAITOR, THERE'S AN ENEMY TO HIS COUNTRY."[55]

---

[54] Morgan, *Stamp Act Crisis*, 121–127.
[55] *Connecticut Courant* [Hartford], September 2, 1765.

Dr. Benjamin Church's pamphlet, *Liberty and Property vindicated, and the St—pm—n burnt,* commemorated this event.[56] It is a satirical oration in the form of a sermon which was purported to have been delivered from Ingersoll's gallows in New London while the effigy burned. There is no evidence to assume however that Church was in New London at the time. He probably wrote the piece after reading newspaper accounts of the event. In the pamphlet Dr. Church presented an allegory between Biblical and contemporary events. He used as his theme the well known story of the golden calf from Exodus, chapter 32. In the allegory he cast William Pitt as Moses since he was in "every way qualified, morally, as Moses was, to lead a people, being endowed with honor, love, truth, and fidelity." Aaron, the leader whom Moses left in his place and who cast the golden calf, naturally symbolized Lord Bute, who led "the people into all manner of corruption."[57]

This corruption was, to Dr. Church, symbolized and crowned by the Stamp Act and the Distributor of Stamps, Jared Ingersoll, "who is an emblem of the molten calf made by Aaron of old in the wilderness." The analogy was not perfect, but Ingersoll could be said to be like "a beast by having a beastly disposition, as indecency, ingratitude, etc., is said to be brutish (in man)." For Ingersoll, having been sent to England as colonial representative, had "most ungratefully betrayed the liberty of his country; and for the sake of a post in the government of no great value, he commenced executioner to the death warrant of it."[58]

Dr. Benjamin Church feared, as did William Smith and Daniel Dulany, that if the Stamp Act were not opposed all American rights and liberties would be lost. With special reference to the Connecticut situation he wrote:

O Connecticut, Connecticut! where is your charter boasted

[56] Boston, 1765. Reprinted: Bailyn, *Pamphlets of the American Revolution,* 588–597.

[57] *Ibid.,* 591–592.

[58] *Ibid.,* 593.

of for ages past; if the beast is worshiped your charter is void and the government put upon the beast's shoulder, who is an ill-bred beast, nursed and brought up to devour you; which must be acknowledged by every friend to liberty and property.

He called upon the people to "stand fast in the liberties granted you by your royal charter" and urged the freemen of Connecticut to defend their rights and privileges. In Dr. Church's opinion actions of this nature could not be labelled as treason or rebellion. He acknowledged the necessity of protecting what he termed "absolute rights" to be fully as demanding as the obligation to protect one's home. If forced, a man could and should protect both as possessions.[59]

Therefore it was those men who supported Great Britain who were guilty of sedition. Foremost among these men was, of course, Jared Ingersoll. Reverting to his allegory Church stated that the people of New London should emulate Moses "and make a sacrifice of the calf, rather than a sacrifice thereunto. Burn it in the fire, grind it to powder, and strow it upon the ocean, that the filthy naughtiness of the beast may be cleansed from the earth." If the burning of the effigy did not enlighten Ingersoll then Dr. Church counselled the use of force to persuade the Distributor of Stamps to resign.

If he willfully persists in his wickedness, use him in such a manner that he will be glad to conform to the truth; and if he is in any post that unjustly grinds the face of the poor or that contributes to your slavery, ask him peaceably to resign it, and if he refuses to, use him in such a manner that he will be glad to do anything for a quiet life. For Britons never must be slaves. . . . Therefore, take care of Mr. St——pm—n, alias the molten calf. AMEN.[60]

About the same time as he wrote *Liberty and Property vin-*

---

[59] *Ibid.*, 594, 596.
[60] *Ibid.*, 595–597.

dicated, and the St——pm—n burnt Benjamin Church also published *The Times A Poem*. Like the pamphlet it commemorated the Stamp Act and condemned the actions of Jared Ingersoll, Lord Bute and George Grenville. In many respects *The Times* is even more vituperative than the pamphlet. Dealing with Ingersoll, Bute and Grenville specifically Church wrote:

Fatigu'd with numbers, and oppress'd with gall,
One general curse must overwhelm them all:
But O ye vilest vile, detested FEW!
Eager, intent, and potent to undoe;
Come out ye parricides! here take your stand.
Your solemn condemnation is at hand;
Behold your crimes, and tremblingly await
The grumbling thunder of your country's hate;
Accursed as you are! how durst ye bring
An injur'd people to distrust their K ——?

Towards the end of the poem Dr. Church castigated Governor Francis Bernard of Massachusetts for his support of the Stamp Act as a

Fop, witling, fav-rite st——pm—n, tyrant, tool,
Of all those mighty names in one, thou fool!
Let mean ambition, sordid lust of pride,
League the vile Pander! to a tryants' side;[61]

Dr. Church's hatred of the Stamp Act and its supporters was more virulent than William Smith's or Daniel Dulany's because of the emotional rather than political orientation of his work. But it cannot be said that it was any less important than the political tracts. As a tool of propaganda satire is probably more effective in reaching large numbers of people than logical argumentation. Church's writings enjoyed a wide circulation and undoubtedly helped to focus and direct the colonial opposition to the Stamp Act.

----

[61] *The Times A Poem* [Boston, 1765], 10–11, 13.

William Samuel Johnson was as strongly opposed to Jared Ingersoll as Benjamin Church and did not disapprove of the methods used by the Sons of Liberty to gain their ends. Although he never explicitly sanctioned what the Tories considered to be the excesses committed by the Sons of Liberty he was, according to Ezra Stiles, a member of that extralegal body in fact, if not in name.[62] When the Connecticut Assembly decided to petition the king and Parliament for the repeal of the Stamp Act, it was William Samuel Johnson who wrote the petitions which were subsequently adopted. The Connecticut Resolves were in most respects similar to the resolves of other colonies. Johnson considered the British constitution to be "the hapiest in the World, founded . . . in the best Manner calculated to secure the Prerogatives of the Crown, while it maintains the just Rights and Liberties of the Subject."[63] He denied the concept of virtual representation and declared that the Stamp Act was "unprecedented and unconstitutional."[64] But Connecticut did not deny the supremacy of the crown. Johnson asked only that the Connecticut charter, issued during the reign of King Charles II, remain in effect. To the Connecticut House of Representatives this charter was "the surest Band of Union, Confidence, and mutual Prosperity of our Mother-Country, and Us, and the best Foundation, on which to build the good of the whole."[65] After writing the resolves, the legislature considered sending Johnson to London as special colonial agent to present its remonstrances.

When news of the passage of the Stamp Act reached Boston, the Massachusetts House of Representatives sent a circular letter to the assemblies of the North American colonies urging them to send delegates to a congress to be held in New York City in October. Nine colonies responded. Georgia, North Caro-

---

[62] Ezra Stiles, *Extracts from the Itineraries . . . with a selection from his Correspondence* (ed. Franklin B. Dexter; New Haven, 1916), 64.
[63] Morgan, *Prologue to Revolution,* 54.
[64] *Ibid.,* 55.
[65] *Ibid.,* 56.

lina and Virginia could not elect delegates because their governors refused to convene their assemblies; New Hampshire declined the invitation. Each of the other colonies sent three delegates. William Samuel Johnson, Eliphalet Dyer, and David Rowland represented Connecticut.[66] The Assembly instructed them to draft a "united, humble, loyal and dutiful representation to his Majesty and Parliament." The delegates were required to submit the resolves and petitions of the congress to the Assembly for final acceptance or rejection.[67]

Timothy Ruggles, a Massachusetts conservative and confidant of Governor Francis Bernard's, was elected chairman of the Stamp Act Congress. Bernard had instructed Ruggles to persuade the meeting to recommend that the colonies submit to the Stamp Act until it was possible to persuade Parliament to repeal it.[68] Ruggles was unable to do this. Let by Christopher Gadsden of South Carolina, John Dickinson of Pennsylvania, and William Samuel Johnson of Connecticut, the delegates drew up a statement delineating the rights and privileges of the colonies.[69] The declarations were moderate in tone. They rejected the argument of virtual representation in the House of Commons, denied the right of Parliament to impose taxes upon the colonies and asserted that trial by jury is the inherent right of every subject in the colonies. From these suppositions they concluded that the Stamp Act "by imposing Taxes on the Inhabitants of these Colonies, and the said Act, and several other Acts, by extending the Jurisdiction of the Courts of Admiralty beyond its ancient Limits, have a manifest Tendency to subvert the Rights and Liberties of the Colonists.[70]

[66] Eben Edwards Beardsley, *Life and Times of William Samuel Johnson, LL. D., first Senator in Congress from Connecticut, and President of Columbia College, New York* (New York, 1876), 32.

[67] *The Public Records of the Colony of Connecticut* (ed. Charles J. Hoadly and J. Hammond Trumbull; 15 vols., Hartford, 1850–1890), XII, 410.

[68] Francis Bernard to Timothy Ruggles, September 28, 1765; Francis Bernard Papers, Harvard College Library.

[69] Morgan, *Stamp Act Crisis*, 103–113.

[70] Morgan, *Prologue to Revolution*, 62–63.

Although William Samuel Johnson acquiesced in the resulting declarations and petitions of the congress, he had hoped for a more general statement of American rights and privileges which would have wider connotations than just the Stamp Act. He wished they "had adopted the other plan of admitting the general superintendence of Parliament and limiting their Power by the Principles and Spirit of the Constitution which sufficiently excludes all Constitutional Right to Tax us, and effectually secures the fundamental Privilege of Trial by Jury as well as every other Right Essential to British Liberty."[71] In a report to the Stamp Act Congress, which is preserved among his papers, he denied the right of Parliament not only to levy internal taxes in the colonies but also external duties. As long as the colonies were not represented in Parliament, neither internal nor external taxes were "consistent with any degree of freedom." Johnson did not deny the supremacy of Parliament over the empire as long as this authority was consistent with the colonists' "Enjoyment of our Essential Rights as Freemen and British Subjects." This "due subordination" to Parliament was guaranteed by the Common Law and by the veto the crown enjoyed over the laws of the colonial legislatures. It meant submission to the British Parliament in matters of legislation but not in matters concerning taxes.[72]

Daniel Dulany had made the same point in *Considerations*. Most Americans at the time of the Stamp Act made a distinction between legislation and taxation. Parliament was sovereign only with regard to legislative suzerainty. Powers of taxation were reserved solely for the colonial legislatures. Since the Stamp Act was an internal tax, most of the colonial opposition to it was concerned with internal taxation. But, at

[71] William Samuel Johnson to Robert Ogden, November 4, 1765; William Samuel Johnson Papers, Connecticut Historical Society.

[72] "Report of the Committee to whom was refer'd the Consideration of the Rights of the British Colonies;" William Samuel Johnson Papers, Library of Congress. This paper constitutes the chief evidence for the Morgans' argument concerning internal and external taxation in *The Stamp Act Crisis*, 114–115.

the same time, to most Americans no distinction existed between internal and external taxes. Both, as the British government was to learn, were considered to be unconstitutional by the colonists.

While William Samuel Johnson was leading the fight against the Stamp Act, Jared Ingersoll was being harassed by the Connecticut Sons of Liberty and was attempting to get the colony to submit to the unpopular measure; a tax which he considered to be eminently fair to the Americans. For, as he pointed out, Great Britain was obliged to maintain an army of seven thousand men on the American frontiers at an annual cost of £300,000. The Stamp Act was expected to raise only one-third of this amount.[73] Americans, he thought, ought to pay a fair share for the contribution that England was making to the defense of the colonies. American ideas about the British constitution and their rights as British subjects which contradicted this were, to Jared Ingersoll, "Notions of Independence."[74] Ingersoll was trying to enforce the Stamp Act at a time when Johnson and the Sons of Liberty were willing "to submit to all the inconveniences of a total stagnation of business rather than admit the act."[75]

When Daniel Dulany's *Considerations* first reached Philadelphia, the opposition to the Stamp Act had already been formulated. Pennsylvania politics revolved around a long standing struggle between the proprietary and the Assembly for control of the province. The Quaker Party had controlled the Assembly for many years because of the over-representation of the eastern counties in the legislature. Although the Penn family was Anglican at the time, they and the Presbyterians were allied in an attempt to limit the influence of the Quakers. As a result, many Presbyterians attained high office under the

---

[73] As "Civis" in the *Connecticut Gazette*, August 9, 1765.

[74] Jared Ingersoll to Richard Jackson, November 3, 1765; Gipson, *Ingersoll*, 193.

[75] William Samuel Johnson to James Otis, November 4, 1765; Beardsley, *William Samuel Johnson*, 195–196.

proprietary government. The leader of the Presbyterian Party, William Allen, became Chief Justice of Pennsylvania. During the year 1764 the Quaker Party, in control of the Assembly and under the leadership of Benjamin Franklin, Joseph Galloway and John Hughes, drew up a petition to the king calling for the establishment of royal government in Pennsylvania. It was hoped that the abolition of the proprietary would leave the Quakers in control of the legislature while the executive office would be in the hands of a royal governor. The Quaker Party hoped that a royal government would be more negligent with regard to Pennsylvania's internal affairs than was the proprietary. The Presbyterians opposed this action and in the election of October, 1764 were able to control the Philadelphia delegation to the Assembly and defeat Franklin and Galloway at the polls, although the Quakers still commanded a majority in the lower house. Benjamin Franklin was sent to England to push the cause of royal government.

The issue of royal government as opposed to the proprietary became submerged in the struggle concerning the Stamp Act. Although Franklin had initially opposed the stamp tax, he did not hesitate to propose his friend John Hughes to Grenville for the post of Distributor of Stamps for Pennsylvania. The high level leadership of the Quaker Party—Franklin, Galloway and Hughes—thereby supported the act. The Presbyterian or Proprietary Party opposed the measure and the Allen family became the leaders of the popular opposition. Provincial politics were such that the Quaker Party, committed to the overthrow of the Penn family, acquiesced in the Stamp Act as a step in the direction of royal government. The Presbyterian Party and the Penns were opposed to the Quaker move and to the Stamp Act as well.[76]

When the Pennsylvania Assembly met in September, 1765, delegates were chosen to attend the Stamp Act Congress des-

[76] Theodore Thayer, *Pennsylvania Politics and the Growth of Democracy 1740–1776* (Harrisburg, Pennsylvania, 1953), 116–125. Morgan, *Stamp Act Crisis*, 238–248.

pite the opposition of John Hughes and the Quaker Party. A committee headed by John Allen, brother of Andrew, and John Dickinson drafted the instructions for the delegation. Later in the month a mass meeting led by James Allen, with Andrew Allen in attendance, demanded Hughes's resignation as Distributor of Stamps. Hughes refused. Then, on October 5th, his commission and the stamps arrived in Philadelphia and a meeting, led by the four Allen brothers—Andrew, James, John and William, Jr.—was held at the state house. According to the Distributor of Stamps, the meeting consisted of "Presbyterians and proprietary Emmissaries with the Chief Justices (Mr. William Allens) Sons at their Head animating and encouraging the lower Class."[77] The mass meeting appointed a delegation led by the Allen brothers, John Dickinson, Charles Thomson, James Tilghman and Robert Morris to wait on Hughes and once again demand his resignation and his promise never to distribute stamps. The Distributor of Stamps refused to resign, but agreed not to attempt to enforce the act until it should be put into effect in the other colonies. At the same time the merchants of Philadelphia, in response to Daniel Dulany's call, unanimously adopted resolutions not to import British goods until the repeal of the Stamp Act. In November the members of the Philadelphia bar, including Andrew Allen, resolved to conduct legal business without the use of stamped paper; only Joseph Galloway and John Ross, leaders of the Quaker Party, opposed the measure.

The Pennsylvania opposition to the Stamp Act had begun as a purely local dispute and the Quaker Party continued, throughout the crisis, to think of it in terms of local politics. Hughes, for example, tried to transform the conflict into an argument in favor of royal government, claiming that the Presbyterians, supported by the proprietary government, were rebels and republicans. They were, he claimed, "as averse to Kings, as they were in the Days of Cromwell" and looked

---

[77] Morgan, *Stamp Act Crisis*, 250.

only to their own selfish interests.[78] But, although the Quaker Party did not recognize the fact, the dispute was not a purely local one. The Presbyterian Party was caught up in a struggle which had implications far more reaching than Pennsylvania provincial politics alone. They recognized the fact that what was at stake was not only control of the Assembly, but the whole concept of empire and colonial unity which they supported along with the Whigs of the other colonies.

The Stamp Act was repealed on March 18, 1766 and the Declaratory Act was signed into law on the same day. News of this "Momentous Event," wrote Daniel Dulany, "diffused the greatest Joy through this Continent."[79] The various colonies sent expressions of gratitude to the king and Parliament. William Samuel Johnson drafted the address of the Connecticut House of Representatives to the king; William Smith and John Morin Scott did likewise in New York at the request of the governor, Council and Assembly. Repeal of the hated measure saw great rejoicing in Philadelphia, although the leaders of the Quaker Party tried to keep the city as quiet as possible. They still thought of the struggle in local terms and did not wish to commemorate the Presbyterian victory. They were unable to stop the celebration, however, for as Joseph Galloway wrote, "the city was illuminated by the proprietary party."[80]

But the leaders of the agitation against the Stamp Act did not feel that everything would now be all right between England and her colonies. Instead they began to search for the fundamental causes as to why Parliament had imposed the obnoxious tax and tried to remove the "traitors" in America from positions of power. Connecticut, in 1766, turned Governor Fitch and four Assistants who had upheld the Stamp Act out of office and elected opponents of the tax in their place. Wil-

---

[78] Ibid., 254.
[79] Daniel Dulany to Lord Baltimore, [1766?], Shelburne Papers, William L. Clements Library, University of Michigan.
[80] Thayer, Pennsylvania Politics, 125.

liam Samuel Johnson became the first Episcopalian to serve
in the Connecticut Council at this election. His election was
attributed to the fact that during the agitation he "politically
became a Son of Liberty."[81]

Johnson believed the Stamp Act had been passed because
members of Parliament were able to obtain little accurate information about America and paid little attention to the problems of these colonists. He hoped that because of the agitation
against the Stamp Act, Parliament hereafter would be "prop-
erly informed of our real Circumstances, & have just Plan's
laid before them." This would be a "good Step . . . towards
restoring Harmony between Great Britain & her Colonies."[82]
And yet Johnson believed that the Grenville ministry had
formulated a "formal design" for the enslavement of America.
"But by pressing it too much and making more haste than
good speed they have defeated the whole design and given
such an Alarm as will forever keep America upon her guard."[83]

Daniel Dulany was sure that the colonies would have to
remain watchful, for on the same day as the Stamp Act had
been repealed, the Declaratory Act had become law. In the
general excitement it had passed virtually unnoticed in the
colonies. However Dulany recognized the act as a threat to
American rights and believed it to be unconstitutional. He
argued that Parliament had no right to tax the colonies despite the Declaratory Act.[84] All the same, America would have
to look to itself for the future and beware of Parliament for,
in the minds of Daniel Dulany, William Samuel Johnson and
William Smith, the Stamp Act had only been one of a series
of measures designed to abridge American rights. They linked
the measure to the creation of stronger Vice-Admiralty Courts

---

[81] Stiles, *Itineraries*, 64.

[82] William Samuel Johnson to John Dickinson, May 24, 1766;
Sparks Mss., Harvard College Library.

[83] William Samuel Johnson to Christopher Gadsden, January 10, 1766;
William Samuel Johnson Papers, Connecticut Historical Society.

[84] Daniel Dulany to Henry Conway, n. d.; Sparks Mss., Harvard
College Library.

and the consequent weakening of trial by jury, as well as to such questions as the emission of legal tender currency and trade regulation.

The crisis caused in America by the Stamp Act was the first act in the drama leading towards the formation of national political ideologies in the American colonies which culminated in civil war and revolution. The political leanings of the colonial oligarchies before this event were concerned primarily with intra-colonial struggles for power and patronage. The events of 1765–1766 led the Whig and Tory oligarchs to take a broader view of the problems facing the British colonists in America. Their response to this first clash with England began the process which formalized two conflicting national political creeds. The response of the socio-political leadership of the colonies to the problems created by the Stamp Act began this process.

Three approaches to the problem can be ascertained in the writings and actions of these men. Two of them led towards a Whig, or patriotic, approach to the forthcoming struggle. Such men as Robert Alexander, William Samuel Johnson, the New York Triumvirate of William Smith, William Livingston and John Morin Scott, the Allen family, Dr. Benjamin Church, and other Whigs such as John Adams viewed the struggle in terms of the limits of Parliament authority over the colonies. To these men, who represented the opposition to the tax, all forms of Parliamentary taxation which concerned the colonies were illegal, unconstitutional and subversive of American rights and liberties. It was at this time that the idea of inherent natural rights as defined by John Locke first made its appearance as a prominent part of the colonists' argument; although William Smith had referred to these rights as early as 1752 in *The Independent Reflector*. At that time few men adopted Smith's position. But when, in 1765, he used a natural rights argument to justify colonial opposition to the Stamp Act the idea began to gain a degree of prominence and im-

portance in Whig thought. Smith and John Morin Scott also
advanced the idea of independence in 1765 if American de-
mands for self-taxation were not met.

These men were willing to use any means within their
power to uphold what they conceived of as their rights and
liberties as British subjects; they were even willing to use
extra-legal bodies such as the Sons of Liberty. Smith and Livingston feared that the mob might get out of hand and believed that mob action could lead to the breakdown of all government. But they were more hostile to the attempts of the
British Parliament to impose its authority and felt, as did the
others, that the use of the mob and force were necessary to
combat the excesses of the English government.[85] All of these
men saw that business would have to proceed as usual without
the use of stamps. For, to close the law courts and curtail business would be an implicit acknowledgment of the authority
of Parliament to tax the colonies, would place an economic
burden on the colonies from which recovery would be difficult
and, in effect, reduce colonial opposition to the level of a petty
attempt to save money through non-taxation.

In the actions of Daniel Dulany can be seen the origins
of what may be called a Whig-Loyalist philosophy. Dulany
was uncompromisingly opposed to the Stamp Act as being
unconstitutional, but he limited his opposition to constitutional
means. Unconstitutional mob action or even action by a colonial legislature tended to subvert the British constitution—
upon which the empire was founded—as much as did the
Stamp Act itself. To Dulany, one was as bad as the other. Although he was probably the first American to propose the
tactics of non-intercourse and the use of homespun as a means
of combatting British imperial policy, this action would be
illegal if proposed or implemented by a colonial legislature.
It could only be instituted if the people themselves thought
of the idea and spread it by example. For a legislature, or any

---

[85] William Smith to Robert Monckton, November 8, 1765; *WS Diary*
I, 30–32.

other organized body, to recommend the action was, in Dulany's opinion, to institute an illegal combination in restraint of trade.

Jared Ingersoll and Thomas Hutchinson represent the origins of a Tory philosophy. Neither of these men was in favor of the Stamp Act and (by their own admission) did all in their power to lessen the duties to be levied upon the colonists. Their opposition to the tax was not a constitutional one but was based solely on economic argumentation. They believed that high duties would curtail business and commerce and defeat the purpose of the act, which was to raise a revenue in America. Both were sure that lower duties would lead to an increased revenue. Once the Stamp Act became law both Hutchinson and Ingersoll attempted to enforce it. They believed that agitation against the act was illegal and subversive. Parliament was the supreme legislative body in the empire and enjoyed supreme power. Thus to the Tory, Parliament had the authority not only to legislate for England and the empire, but also to regulate trade and impose taxes on all parts of the empire. Any colonial opposition to the doctrine of Parliamentary supremacy was aimed at independence because it, if effective, would tend to lessen English control over all parts of the empire.

Thus three bodies of political thought began their development in the pre-revolutionary era. One of these groups was willing to use any means in its power to oppose what its members considered to be the illegal machinations of Parliament. Another opposed Parliament on constitutional grounds and believed that the means of protest used by the colonists must conform to constitutional principles. The third upheld the supremacy of Parliament over the empire and believed that any opposition to this supremacy was subversive and tended towards independence.

3

TARIFFS AND TAXES

During the relatively quiet period from 1766 to 1771 the future Whig-Loyalists continued to be identified with the Whigs against the Tories. Some, such as William Smith, William Samuel Johnson, Dr. Benjamin Church and Robert Alexander became more prominent politically, while the ideological leader of the Stamp Act opposition, Daniel Dulany, began to decline into a relatively insignificant position. Why this came about can be attributed to the changing nature of the struggle between Great Britain and her American colonies during these years. In their elation over the repeal of the Stamp Act most Americans had paid little attention to the Declaratory Act. They were soon to learn however that the repeal of the Stamp Act had not ended the conflict with England. The Quartering Act of 1765 (extended in 1766) remained in effect and in 1767 the Townshend Acts were passed which brought the struggle for colonial rights to the fore once again. This was to lead to a revival of non-importation agreements in the colonies.

The colonial policy pursued by George Grenville included not only the idea of raising a revenue in the colonies but also, to alleviate the heavy burden of empire expenditures incurred in England, to establish in the colonies some regiments of the British Army. He therefore proposed, and Parliament passed, "An Act for punishing Mutiny and Desertion, and for the better Payment of the Army and their Quarters." The act stated that in the absence of barracks in any colony where it was necessary to station troops, the province should be responsible for providing adequate quarters for the troops in uninhabited houses, inns and livery stables. In addition the colony was required to provide the soldiers with bedding, firewood, cooking utensils, candles, salt and alcoholic beverages.

In accordance with the provisions of the act General Thomas Gage asked Sir Henry Moore, Royal Governor of New York, to make provision for those of his troops who were stationed in the province. There was little opposition in New York to the establishment of troops in the colony, in fact New York with its extensive frontier welcomed them. But the requirement of the act that the colony must pay for the support of the troops was deemed to be a direct tax disguised as a requisition. And so, even though Governor Moore transmitted General Gage's request to the Assembly on December 3rd, it was not until July 3, 1766 that the request was acted upon and then only after the Assembly had passed a series of resolutions opposing implementation of the Quartering Act. The act that was finally passed provided quarters for the troops but made no mention of salt or beverages. This the Assembly justfied by stating that these last articles were not furnished to troops in English barracks. This non-compliance with the Quartering Act was not based solely on a refusal to provide the necessary funds, but on political and constitutional objections to the act as well. New York had always been willing to provide money for the army. For example, on July 2, 1766, just one day prior to the passage of the act to provide quarters, the Assembly resolved that whenever troops should, at the request of the governor and with the consent of the Council, march to any part of the colony it would provide the necessary funds. The Assembly acknowledged that when the crown applied for aid the colony should obey, but in the act it passed on July 3rd the Assembly ignored the Quartering Act and implied that Parliament had no right to interfere in what was essentially a matter for the crown and the colony to decide.

Parliament, understandably, was far from satisfied with the conduct of the New York Assembly. The king vetoed the act of July 3rd and Parliament considered it to be little better than an open refusal to comply with the Quartering Act. Accordingly, Parliament passed the Restraining Act which suspended the New York Assembly until such time as "provision shall have been made for furnishing the King's troops with all the necessaries required by law."[1]

The conflict in New York over the Quartering Act soon merged into the struggle with England over the so-called Townshend revenue acts. When taken as a whole the Quartering Act, Restraining Act and Townshend Acts were viewed in the colonies with some trepidation. It was feared, with perhaps some justification, that taxation as represented by the Stamp Act and Townshend Acts was merely the preliminary to the complete suppression of any degree of legislative independence in the colonies.

William Samuel Johnson had been sent to London by Connecticut in 1766 as colonial agent.[2] From his observations of the English political scene he came to the conclusion that "the less they [Parliament] think, or we give them occasion to think of us, I imagine the better for us."[3] He had discovered that American affairs were brought up in the House of Commons as a method, used by the opposition, of attacking the

---

[1] On the Quartering Act, its passage and effects, see: Gipson, *British Empire*, XI, 39–69; and Becker, *Political Parties*, 53–58.

[2] *Public Records of the Colony of Connecticut*, XII, 501.

[3] William Samuel Johnson to William Pitkin, March 19, 1767; Bancroft Transcripts, William Samuel Johnson Correspondence, New York Public Library.

ministry as the supposed friend of the colonists.[4] Johnson also found to his amazement that most members of Parliament believed "that America is aiming at an immediate independency on this country and in consequence of this mistaken opinion they think it necessary to vindicate their supremacy and insist upon an implicit obedience to the dictates of this Legislature." He warned that this might lead to measures being taken against the colonies and pointed to the suspension of the New York Assembly by Parliament, for failure to comply with the Quartering Act, as proof of his point.[5]

Johnson's surmise was correct, for when Charles Townshend became Chancellor of the Exchequer he introduced several pieces of legislation affecting the colonies. Although William Samuel Johnson never gained access to the more important Parliamentary leaders, he displayed a remarkable propensity for obtaining news of the proposed measures, even at the risk of his own official position in London. All the provincial agents had been excluded from the House of Commons during debate on the colonies, but Johnson managed to secret himself in the galleries on May 15 when Grenville spoke against the Americans.[6] In a letter written to Governor William Pitkin of Connecticut he described the proceedings and was able to give an exact account of the measures which were to be passed.[7]

The Townshend Revenue Act and another measure which received the royal assent on the same day set up an American Board of Commissioners of the Customs at Boston with jurisdiction over all customs officials in the American colonies. It was to be responsible only to the British Treasury Board.

---

[4] William Samuel Johnson to William Pitkin, April 11, 1767; *ibid.*

[5] *Ibid.* William Samuel Johnson to Samuel Gray, June 9, 1767; Bancroft Transcripts, Connecticut Papers. See also: William Samuel Johnson to William Pitkin, June 9, 1767; *Trumbull Papers,* 236.

[6] Groce, *William Samuel Johnson,* 73.

[7] William Samuel Johnson to William Pitkin, May 16, 1767; *Trumbull Papers,* 233.

In 1768 a further measure divided America into four districts, each with a Vice-Admiralty Court. These were to be located at Halifax, Boston, Philadelphia and Charleston and were to have the power not only to hear appeals from the colonial Vice-Admiralty Courts, but also to have original jurisdiction in some cases.

Jared Ingersoll was rewarded for his stand on the Stamp Act by being appointed a judge of the Vice-Admiralty Court at Philadelphia with an annual salary of £400.[8] Ingersoll had no objection to the import duties which were laid upon the colonies. They were "as well chosen as any could be" and there would not, in his opinion, be any "grumbling about the matter" in the colonies.[9] Thomas Hutchinson took somewhat the same view. He was not in favor of the new taxes and thought that they were inexpedient. But he had no doubts as to the legality of the measures and believed that they should be enforced. Hutchinson apparently thought that the colonies should submit to the new tax rather than break the connection with England. Like the members of Parliament William Samuel Johnson had interviewed, Hutchinson believed that independence was a distinct possibility if the Townshend Acts were opposed with the same vigor as had been displayed by the opposition to the Stamp Act.[10] Thus the Tory viewpoint at this time was that although it might not, in view of the recent opposition to the Stamp Act, be expedient to levy taxes upon the colonies, there was no objection to them on legal or moral grounds. If Parliament saw fit to levy taxes then it was the duty of the colonists to submit. The Whig view of the controversy was quite the opposite.

The most impressive and significant attack upon the Town-

---

[8] Gipson, *Ingersoll*, 294–295.

[9] Jared Ingersoll to William Samuel Johnson, July 23, 1767; William Samuel Johnson Papers, Connecticut Historical Society.

[10] James Kendall Hosmer, *The Life of Thomas Hutchinson Royal Governor of the Province of Massachusetts Bay* (Boston and New York, 1896), 124. Brown, *Middle Class Democracy*, 241.

shend duties came from the pen of John Dickinson of Pennsylvania in his famous *Letters from a Farmer in Pennsylvania to the Inhabitants of the British Colonies* which were widely reprinted in pamphlet form.[11] In many respects John Dickinson's career paralleled that of Daniel Dulany. Dulany, the ideological leader of the Stamp Act opposition, became a conservative as the crisis with England matured and eventually became a Loyalist. He would not accept the decision in Congress of July 4, 1776. Dickinson became the ideological leader of the opposition to the Townshend duties and like Dulany had his doubts about the efficacy of independence. During the 1760's he was allied with the Allen family in Pennsylvania and was a leading radical. Yet by 1776, although he eventually acquiesced in independence, there was little to differentiate his views from those of such Whig-Loyalists as William Smith, William Samuel Johnson or Andrew Allen.

In the twelve *Farmer's Letters* John Dickinson admitted the right of Parliament to regulate, and even suppress, the commerce and industry of the colonies. These regulations might even produce an incidental revenue. But he denied that Parliament had the authority to levy either internal or external taxes upon the colonies. Dickinson's statements provided the ideological basis for opposition to the Townshend Acts much as Dulany's pamphlet had done for the Stamp Act. His stand differed from the earlier Whig statement primarily in his strong rejection of the concept of external taxation. Dulany had rejected both internal and external taxes but had admitted the right of Parliament to regulate the trade of the Empire. Dickinson did much the same thing. But due to the difference in the nature of the struggle in 1765 and 1768, they stressed different points. Since the Stamp Act had levied an internal tax, Dulany placed primary emphasis on demonstrating the unconstitutionality of internal taxation and had denied the concept of virtual representation. John Dickinson wrote in op-

---

[11] First appeared in the *Pennsylvania Chronicle and Universal Advertiser,* December 2, 1767 to February 17, 1768.

position to a Parliamentary attempt to lay revenue-producing tariffs on American commerce and thereby stressed the unconstitutionality of external taxation. Practical opposition to the Townshend acts came through the use of commercial retaliation as a weapon in the constitutional struggle against the government of Great Britain. It was natural then that Whigs and Tories showed their feelings by either supporting or rejecting the non-importation agreements.

The Whigs agreed that the Townshend Acts were, if not unconstitutional, then at least detrimental to the commercial and industrial growth of America. In order to make their resentment known the colonists revived Daniel Dulany's plan for the non-importation of British goods. From England William Samuel Johnson sent back a running commentary on the effects that the non-importation agreements were having upon the mother country and made suggestions about how non-importation could be improved. These letters constitute a clear expression of the Whig position on non-importation during this period.[12] Learning of the pending duties even before they had passed the House of Commons, Johnson immediately began to recommend that Americans think about the non-consumption of taxed items. Writing specifically about tea he concluded that it would be "wise" if Americans were "to substitute in lieu of this expensive exotic, some of the more salutary herbs of their own country."[13] He later extended this argument to include all manufactures from Great Brtiain and advocated the self-sufficiency of America.[14] Johnson urged that non-importation measures be stringently enforced, believ-

---

[12] These letters may be found in the Connecticut Historical Society and the Bancroft Transcripts. For a summery of Johnson's political philosophy in the era see: Evarts Boutell Greene, "William Samuel Johnson and the American Revolution," *Columbia University Quarterly*, XXII, 1930, 157–178.

[13] William Samuel Johnson to William Pitkin, June 9, 1767; Bancroft Transcripts, William Samuel Johnson Correspondence.

[14] William Samuel Johnson to Joseph Trumbull, April 15, 1769; *Trumbull Papers*, 333.

ing that the safety of America depended upon "those salutary agreements."[15]

As an American patriot in London William Samuel Johnson was somewhat more radical than was Benjamin Franklin. Franklin had supported the Stamp Act but when he perceived the American reaction to it became a moderate Whig and worked for its repeal. In February, 1766 he was asked by the House of Commons whether there was "any kind of difference between the two taxes [internal and external] to the Colony on which they are laid?" He replied that there was a great difference.

An external tax is a duty laid on commodities imported . . . and, when it is offered for sale, makes a part of the price. If the people do not like it at that price, they refuse it; they are not obliged to pay it. But an internal tax is forced upon the people without their consent, if not laid by their own representatives.[16]

Franklin therefore did not consider external taxes to be unconstitutional and maintained the distinction between internal and external taxation for the purpose of raising a revenue. But after the publication of the *Farmer's Letters* he abandoned this distinction and worked "to obtain a repeal as general as possible of all American revenue acts." In the meantime he hoped that nothing would occur in the colonies "to change the favourable sentiments toward us which apparently begin to take place in the minds of his Majesty and his ministers."[17] It therefore seems as if Benjamin Franklin acted in response

---

[15] William Samuel Johnson to William Pitkin, September 18, 1769; Bancroft Transcripts, William Samuel Johnson Correspondence. See also: William Samuel Johnson to William Pitkin, July 23, 1768, May 25, 1769; *Trumbull Papers*, 291, 348–349.

[16] *The Writings of Benjamin Franklin* (ed. Albert Henry Smyth; 10 vols., New York, 1905–1907), IV, 424.

[17] Benjamin Franklin to Noble Wymberley Jones, Speaker of the Georgia Assembly, June 7, 1769; *Benjamin Franklin's Autobiographical Writings* (ed. Carl Van Doren; New York, 1945), 190–191.

to American events and did not attempt to influence them
as did William Samuel Johnson.

Johnson, from his vantage point in London, and many other
Whigs in the colonies immediately perceived what Franklin
did not: that the greatest threat from the Townshend acts was
not the fact that they laid taxes upon the colonies but, in
Johnson's words, from

> that part of them which enables his Majesty to apply the
> produce of these duties towards *defraying the charges of*
> *the administration of justice and the support of the civil*
> *government within all or any of the Plantations.* By this
> regulation, the Governors will be rendered independent of
> the people, and, wanting no support from them, will have
> very little inducement to call the Assemblies together; nay,
> in time, and it may be feared very soon, the King's govern-
> ment will all become sinecures.[18]

William Samuel Johnson believed, as did most American
Whigs, that the Townshend duties were unconstitutional and
therefore an assault upon American liberty, much as the
Stamp Act had been. But a new facet had now been added:
by allowing the duties to be applied to colonial administration, the Townshend Acts became a two-barrelled threat to
liberty and a further violation of American rights. Therefore,
Johnson believed, opposition to the new measures must be un-
remitting to force their repeal. William Samuel Johnson firmly
believed in the necessity of a supreme political power in the
British empire and Parliament was in the best position to
fulfill this function. But if Parliament were to exercise sov-
ereignty some safeguards must be erected to insure the colonists the free enjoyment of their rights and liberties as citizens
of the British empire. Without safeguards colonial rights
could and would be destroyed, as had been displayed by the
Stamp Act and the current Townshend Acts. However, this

---

18 William Samuel Johnson to William Pitkin, July 13, 1767; *Trumbull*
Papers, 239.

argument created another problem for the Connecticut agent. He perceived in the conflict between colonial rights and Parliamentary supremacy the seeds of the destruction of the British empire. Parliament would try to enforce her supremacy; America would insist upon her rights. Only moderation by men on both sides of the Atlantic would end the conflict and restore harmony within the empire. Johnson therefore advised his correspondents to be cautious in their efforts to maintain colonial rights and urged them towards moderation in order to maintain the empire. This did not mean that they should not protect themselves or oppose the measures Parliament passed, but that the colonial opposition should be based on constitutional arguments and have the force of law.[19]

Robert Alexander was another man who was to become a Whig-Loyalist and supported the opposition to the Townshend Acts. However no statement of his ideological beliefs has survived for this period. They must be inferred from his known actions in Baltimore. In November, 1769 Alexander signed the agreement of the "Associators for the Non-importation of European Goods" at Baltimore. Although there is no evidence that the attorney also engaged in mercantile trade, the association was open to all of the inhabitants of Baltimore County. At a meeting held by the association on November 14, 1769, Alexander proved himself to be more radical than a majority of the associators. The meeting had been called to decide the fate of a cargo of goods, valued at £900, which had arrived in Baltimore from London. The owner of the cargo, William Moore, Jr., claimed that the goods were not purchased in violation of the non-importation agreement, of which he was a signer, and that upon his signing the agreement he had been informed that he would be permitted to purchase a cargo of goods to be imported in the autumn of 1769. The associators unanimously agreed that the cargo had been imported con-

---

[19] See for example: William Samuel Johnson to Joseph Trumbull, April 15, 1769; *Trumbull Papers*, 333.

trary to the non-importation agreement. But when a vote was taken on Moore's plea for an exemption and permission to land and sell the cargo, a majority of the associators voted to permit Moore to do so. Robert Alexander voted in the negative. What good were the agreements and how could England be convinced to repeal the Townshend duties if exemptions were to be allowed? He considered any cargo from England, no matter when or how ordered, to violate the agreements.[20] It can therefore be assumed that Robert Alexander was an uncompromising radical in 1769 and strongly committed to the colonial cause.

William Samuel Johnson was sure that non-importation was not the only method which could be used to defeat the extra-legal machinations of the British government. He was incensed with the thought that since the non-importation agreements were dependent upon the attitudes of the colonial merchants they could be, and were, widely violated. He knew from his own mercantile investments that it was not in the interests of the merchants to support non-importation. To do so they deprived themselves of their livelihood. Johnson believed that only in New York, where the Whig Party was firmly under the control of the New York Triumvirate, were the agreements not infringed upon to any great extent.[21] It was therefore essential to have the people of the colonies take a leading role in keeping the non-importation resolutions intact. As he put it:

Why should this depend upon the merchants only, whose interest it must be to continue that trade by which they acquire wealth? They have, indeed, shown a noble disinterested spirit, which does them great honor; but is not the true ground this, *that the people cease to consume?*

---

[20] Johnson, *Robert Alexander*, 34–35. Scharf, *Chronicles of Baltimore*, 65.

[21] William Samuel Johnson to ?, April 14, 1770; Samuel Johnson Papers, Columbia University Library.

There both interest and duty will concur, and the ground will be absolutely sure. The merchants *must* cease to import if the people will not purchase.[22]

In order for such a policy to succeed, Johnson believed that American opposition to the Townshend measures had to have a firm constitutional basis. In this he was at one with most Whigs of the period. The colonies must present a united front to the measures in order to assure that American rights would be the basis of American relations with Great Britain. These rights must include the provision that John Dickinson had expounded in the *Farmer's Letters*: Any act which had as its purpose the raising of a revenue must be opposed by the colonies as unconstitutional. As Johnson wrote, even if the duty was insignificant,

> it is still an actual exercise of the right of taxation which they claim, and constitutes a precedent against them, in which the Colonies cannot consistent with their principles or rights acquiesce. It is not, I apprehend, the amount of the duties . . . that is the chief ground of the dispute, but the nature and purpose of them. The principle on which they are founded, alone, is worth contesting. A tax of a penny is equally a tax as one of a pound; if they have a constitutional right to impose the first, they may the last; and if they continue the one, with the acquiescence of the Colonies . . . upon the ground of that precedent once admitted and established, they will impose the other also.[23]

William Samuel Johnson's skill in presenting the American position in England and his advice to the colonies received such approbation in his home colony of Connecticut that William Williams, a radical leader and later a signer of the Declaration of Independence, declared that Johnson was likely

[22] William Samuel Johnson to William Pitkin, February 19, 1769; *Trumbull Papers*, 318–319.
[23] William Samuel Johnson to William Pitkin, May 25, 1769; *ibid.*, 349–350.

to be elected the next governor of the colony even though he was a member of the Episcopalian Church.[24] Although this prediction was erroneous, Johnson was considered to be the finest spokesman of the colonial cause that Connecticut produced in the period.[25]

Daniel Dulany approached the constitutional problem which developed with the passage of the Townshend Acts in a different way than Dickinson or Johnson had. He opposed the acts, but his opposition was in conformity with the constitutional opinions he had formulated at the time of the Stamp Act. In all parts of America and England Dulany was associated with opposition to Parliamentary authority. In Virginia the Sons of Saint Patrick toasted him as a champion of freedom, as did John Wilkes's visitors in his jail cell in England.[26] But Dulany never played an active role in the belated Maryland opposition to the Townshend duties. Although he explicitly approved of non-importation and had even been the first to expound the measure, he recoiled from its practical consequences. He considered the agreements to be illegal combinations in restraint of trade as he had at the time of the Stamp Act. All opposition on the basis of non-importation or non-consumption must be by the individual, as an individual action. This opposition was on a theoretical plane and in keeping with the doctrine of a decentralized empire which he had first formulated in *Considerations*. Each part of the empire

[24] William Williams to William Samuel Johnson, July 5, 1768; Bancroft Transcripts, William Samuel Johnson Correspondence.

[25] The election of Johnson as an Assistant in 1766 and the letter by Williams show the regard which the radicals had for Johnson in this period. Anglicans were suspect in the colony and were considered to be supporters of the English position on colonial rights. That Johnson was able to win the support of the radicals is a tribute to his political acumen and lends strong support to the argument that his political aims and ideology were in harmony with those of the Sons of Liberty. On the problem of the Anglicans in Connecticut see: Eben Edwards Beardsley, *History of the Episcopal Church in Connecticut* (2 vols., New York, 1865–1868.)

[26] Land, *Dulanys of Maryland*, 287.

was to have autonomous control over its internal affairs and regulate them through its own legislature. The various parts of the empire were, according to Dulany's constitutional theories, subject to the general overlordship of the King in Parliament. As he wrote in 1768:

> Maryland is no part of the realm or kingdom of *England*, but is a part of its royalty, or of the dominions belonging to it. . . . The people of *Maryland* are the subjects of the King of England, but not his subjects of or in the realm or in the kingdom of England, but in the dominions belonging to it.[27]

From this one can deduce that although Parliament could legislate for the empire, it could not legislate for each individual part of it. Therefore it could not impose taxes on the colonies. Taxes must be imposed only by the several legislatures.

Daniel Dulany's silence at the time of the Townshend Acts, compared with his vigor at the time of the Stamp Act, may be attributed to several causes. Since his legalistic mind recoiled from the idea of non-importation associations, he found various reasons for remaining inactive. His personal affairs were in an uncertain state. As provincial Secretary, Dulany had had a personal understanding with Cecilius Calvert, the principal Secretary, who died in October, 1765, as to the fees he was to receive for his work. But in 1766 he was forced to work out an agreement with the new Secretary, Hugh Hammersley, as to the fees and perquisites of his office. Since the provincial Secretary deputized for the principal Secretary in the colony, these were split between the two men by agreement. Dulany was also involved in delicate negotiations with the proprietor to bring his brother Walter into the provincial government.[28] Since he took no part in mercantile activities, Dulany did not participate in either the Baltimore non-impor-

---

27 *Ibid.*
28 *Ibid.*, 277–280.

tation agreement or the Maryland Association, but his brother-in-law, Christopher Lowndes of Bladensburg, was a leading member of both. A committee to which Lowndes belonged paid tribute to Dulany for his authorship of the non-importation policy.[29] By his silence, and his family's participation in the Association, Dulany was able to maintain his position as a champion of American liberty while privately deploring the practical consequences of the policy which he had first advocated.

The seizure of John Hancock's sloop *Liberty* by the Customs Commissioners on June 10, 1768 and the landing of British troops in Boston in October of the same year incensed the Whigs and for the first time made military coercion an aspect of the struggle. The *Liberty* had been seized for alleged violations of the Townshend Acts and the seizure was therefore considered to be a violation of American rights by the Whigs. However many Whigs—William Samuel Johnson was one—were annoyed by the riots which occurred in Boston protesting the seizure of the aptly named *Liberty*. Nevertheless Johnson disliked the British action as much as did the mob and believing the Townshend duties to be unconstitutional, thought the seizure to be illegal. However in his view mob action could have no good result. Educated men everywhere would look upon this type of response to British measures as leading towards anarchy and would lower the tone of American opposition to the Townshend duties to the level of mere "trifling squabbles." The Bostonians had "exposed themselves to Infinite Ridicule" in England and had, in Johnson's view, hindered the efforts of Americans in London, such as himself, to advance the American cause.[30]

William Samuel Johnson viewed the events in Boston in

[29] *Ibid.*, 237–238.
[30] William Samuel Johnson to Eliphalet Dyer, June 6, 1769; William Samuel Johnson to Jared Ingersoll, January 2, 1769; William Samuel Johnson Papers, Connecticut Historical Society.

June, 1768 from a London perspective. It is not surprising
that a Bostonian, Dr. Benjamin Church, viewed these same
events with somewhat less detachment. Doctor Church believed, as he wrote to the English champion of liberty John
Wilkes, that the riots accompanying the seizure of the *Liberty*
and the military occupation of Boston by elements of the
British army were in keeping with "the liberal Principles of
ancient Britons" and therefore applauded the actions of the
mob. He perceived in the rioting "incontestible Proofs of our
inflexible Firmness and intrepidity when that first, best, dearest
Object, *our Freedom,* is in Jeopardy."[31] Doctor Church supported and helped lead the opponents of military occupation.
He was later to be a member of the committee sent to Lieutenant Governor Hutchinson by the Boston Town Meeting
to protest against the action of the British troops during the
Boston Massacre and to demand that Captain Preston and his
men, the perpetuators of the Massacre, be tried for murder.[32]

William Smith also took a radical view, similar to that of
Benjamin Church, of these actions. He bitterly complained
when the people of New York "saw Boston in the Hands of
an Army yet not one Step was to be taken in Vindication of the
Liberties of the Colonies."[33] Smith was also incensed when
the occasion was not used by New York for further defiance
of Great Britain over the matter of quartering troops in the
colony. He blamed this inaction on the influence of the De-
Lancey faction which, he believed, had taken the side of
England in this quarrel.[34] In this Smith was probably correct
as the DeLanceys became New York's leading Tories. When
the New York Assembly voted to grant a supply for the quartering of troops, Smith denounced them for having betrayed
the people of Boston "who for their glorious Zeal in the Cause

---

[31] Benjamin Church to John Wilkes, July 11, 1769; *Proceedings* of
the Massachusetts Historical Society, XLVII, 204.

[32] Allen French, *General Gage's Informers* (Ann Arbor, Michigan,
1932), 148.

[33] Diary entry, April 4, 1769; *WS Diary* I, 66–67.

[34] *Ibid.*

of American Liberty . . . had their Metropolis converted into a garrisoned town."[35] Smith meanwhile did all he could to delay and obstruct the implementation of the grant.[36]

When New York granted the appropriation required by the Quartering Act, Alexander MacDougall, a leader of the Sons of Liberty in New York, issued a broadside entitled *To the Betrayed Inhabitants of the City and Colony of New York*, criticizing the action of the Assembly. The New York Council, with William Smith in attendance, censured the anonymous handbill as being libelous. When it was discovered that Mac-Dougall was the author, he was arrested. Smith was asked to aid the prosecution in the case but, although he had pressed for MacDougall's prosecution, he refused, saying that he did not wish to serve in an unpopular cause.[37]

On the surface William Smith acted as a loyal member of the Council, but he was playing a double role in this affair. It might be said that he was an *agent provocateur*, for in the Council he had instigated the search into the identity and prosecution of the author of the provocative pamphlet.[38] Yet his friend and partner John Morin Scott served as MacDougall's defense counsellor and Smith himself defended MacDougall's cause in an anonymous letter which was published in the *New York Gazette*.[39] It is perhaps significant that James Parker, the publisher of the *Gazette*, also printed MacDougall's pamphlet. Smith's reasons for having encouraged MacDougall's arrest and prosecution become very clear when reading the first paragraph of this letter.

---

[35] Diary entry, November 29, 1769; *ibid.*, 70.
[36] Diary entry, May 2, 1772; *ibid.*, 123–124.
[37] Diary entry, February 28, 1770; *ibid.*, 75.
[38] Diary entry, January 23, 1770; *ibid.*, 72–73.
[39] "Copy of a late Letter from an eminent Councellor & a Friend to Liberty to his Correspondent in this City," *New York Gazette*, March 19, 1770. At the time it was written the letter was ascribed to John Dickinson, but the original draft of the letter has been found by William H. W. Sabine to be in Smith's handwriting. Apparently Smith tried to make it appear as if a non-New Yorker had written the letter so that its influence would not be associated with the Whig Party in New York.

I rejoice at the Attack upon Capt. McDougal.—Whatever
was the Design of your old Lieut Govr. [Colden] & his
Adherents in stirring up a Prosecution against that gallant
Son of Liberty it will rather advance than injure the grand
Cause of America—The stroke meant at him will prove to
be a fatal one to the Mutiny Act for a spirit of Jelousy &
Enquiry is gone forth and no future wheedling to procure
fresh Compliances with that Statute will succeed. Before
this Alarm our Zeal for Liberty began to languish, Uni-
formity of Sentiment induced a degree of Stupidity & every
Man trusted to the Vigilance of his Neighbour. We were all
composing ourselves for a Nap of Security—There was a
necessity for fresh Oil to quicken that expiring Lamp. . . .
Certainly we should be forward in a sort of Thanks to Mr.
Colden & the Politicians of his Train.—They have done a
good Service to the Continent in sending a Son of Liberty
to Jail.[40]

William Smith's double role in the MacDougall affair thereby
takes on a Machiavellian aspect. Not content to let affairs
take their due course, he pushed for MacDougall's prosecution so as to arouse the people of New York to the threat that
British legislation held for the colony. By doing so he was
able to further his ideas of empire and took a step towards
the autonomy of American internal affairs.

Of more immediate significance to the colonies as a whole
than the MacDougall affair was the advent of Lord North as
Prime Minister in January, 1770. He proposed a bill which
repealed the Townshend duties on all articles except tea. This
act became law on April 12, 1770. At the same time North
pledged that no new taxes would be laid upon the colonies
and allowed the Quartering Act to expire without suggesting
its renewal. The partial repeal of the Townshend duties split
the colonial opposition to England. Although Thomas Hutchinson warned the government that partial repeal would not

---

40 *Ibid.*

help the situation in America, because the colonists would demand the repeal of all taxes and all restraints on trade,[41] deep cracks soon began to appear in the façade America presented to England.

William Samuel Johnson warned just two days after the repeal that America had to remain united and firm in her opposition to Parliament if the Americans were to succeed in achieving what he considered to be the constitutional rights of the colonies. From London he advised that the non-importation measures be retained until the tax on tea was repealed.[42] But although Boston attempted to retain them, various parts of the country began to import British goods in violation of the associations. In July, 1770 New York Ctiy decided to resume importation and Philadelphia followed suit on September 20th. The radical members of the Non-importation Association resigned in protest when the motion to continue non-importation lost by a two to one vote. Prominent among these radicals was the Attorney General of the Commonwealth, Andrew Allen.[43] Boston was forced to follow suit in October because of the actions of New York and Philadelphia. Non-importation was doomed in America even though Virginia held out until July, 1771. Many Whigs were not satisfied with the partial repeal of the Townshend Acts and urged the continuation until the tax was removed from the consumption of tea. Among them were several men who were later to become Loyalists; notably William Samuel Johnson, Andrew Allen, and probably Robert Alexander, Benjamin Church and William Smith.[44]

The year 1771 was one of the most peaceful in these long years of conflict. During it tension between the colonies and

---

[41] Brown, *Middle Class Democracy*, 260.

[42] Extract of a letter by William Samuel Johnson, April 14, 1770; Samuel Johnson Papers, Columbia University Library.

[43] Thayer, *Pennsylvania Politics*, 148.

[44] The opinions of Daniel Leonard, Benjamin Church, Peter Van Schaack and William Byrd III are difficult to determine.

the mother country began to ease. The sole remaining signs of the struggle which had engaged the attention of most men on both sides of the Atlantic were a few agreements in the colonies not to import or use duted tea. This was a minor inconvenience to most Americans who, like John Adams, preferred drinking smuggled tea but who really did not care whether the small duty had been paid or not.[45]

However the response to the Townshend duties in the colonies was of great significance to the development of political ideology in British North America. Loyalist ideology was not changed, but was strengthened by the Tory support of England in this crisis. To the Tories the position was fundamentally the same as that which had confronted them at the time of the Stamp Act. They supported the English measures, although many such as Thomas Hutchinson believed them to be impolitic. To the Tories there was never any question of the legality of the measures. The King in Parliament had the right to legislate for the colonies in any fashion he so desired as the supreme power in the empire. They therefore advised submission to the powers of legitimacy and opposed non-importation as illegal and tending to subvert royal government in America.

The Whigs and those men who later became Whig-Loyalists took the opposite view. Their political ideology at the time was based on the writings of John Dickinson, just as at the time of the Stamp Act they had based their views on the writings of Daniel Dulany. In conformity with Dickinson's view that Parliament could regulate the trade and relationships of the empire but had no authority to tax or legislate for its various parts, most if not all Whigs believed the Townshend duties to be unconstitutional. Conforming to this principle of constitutionality William Samuel Johnson advocated legal opposition to the duties but would not condone mob action or violence. William Smith and Daniel Dulany took differing

---

[45] Diary entry, February 14, 1771; *The Works of John Adams*, II, 255.

positions. Smith and his partners, William Livingston and John Morin Scott, were more radical than most and tried to push events in New York to a logical conclusion by using the MacDougall affair as a lever to force the government to back down on the enforcement of the Quartering Act and the Townshend duties. Dulany's views leaned towards the other direction. While he explicitly approved of non-importation, he recoiled from its practical consequences. Non-importation agreements were, to Dulany, illegal; he could not fight fire with fire and did not believe that what he considered to be illegal methods should be used to fight even an unconstitutional act. Opposition must be carried on solely by legitimate means. Presumably he favored private, voluntary abstinence from British imports.

Thus in the period from 1766 to 1771 we find that there was no difference between Whigs and Whig-Loyalist ideology on such questions as taxation or the regulation of trade. At the time men did not distinguish between the positions taken by such men as William Smith or William Livingston, William Samuel Johnson or James Otis. They saw only a dichotomy of views between radical, moderate and conservative Whigs. Daniel Dulany and James Duane of New York are examples of the latter group while Otis, Johnson, John Adams and others were considered to be moderates. Such men as the New York Triumvirate were radicals. From each of these groups came Patriots and Whig-Loyalists. Yet as late as 1771 there was no method of distinguishing one group from the other.

4

THE BISHOPRIC CONTROVERSY

The controversy over taxation was the primary factor in the development of political ideology in the period from 1766 to 1771, but other matters helped to shape the Whig, Whig-Loyalist and Tory positions. Among these was the controversy over establishment of an American bishopric of the Church of England. The conclusion of the French and Indian War had led England to look at her American colonies with new eyes. Until 1763 the British government had been too occupied with foreign affairs to attend to anything else, but with the end of the war the government was able to give attention to domestic and colonial matters. We have seen how this manifested itself in political affairs. Americans feared, or hoped, that a similar result would atend ecclesiastical matters. Some Episcopal churchmen hoped to found in the American colonies an ecclesiastical organization similar to that of the mother country.[1] But most of the mainland colonies had been founded

[1] For a discussion of this problem see: Arthur Lyon Cross, *The Anglican Episcopate and the American Colonies* (London and New York, 1902) and Carl Bridenbaugh, *Mitre and Sceptre: Transatlantic Faiths, Ideas, Personalities and Politics 1689–1775* (New York, 1962). Alan Heimert, *Religion and the American Mind from the Great Awakening to the Revolution* (Cambridge, Massachusetts, 1966) treats this controversy as "something of a red herring," an artificial issue diverting attention from the real dispute between Evangelicals and Rationalists. The

by groups which were opposed to the Church of England, such as the Catholic Baltimore family, the Puritans of New England, or the Quakers of Pennsylvania. It was primarily in these areas that the Anglicans, as a minority group, supported the establishment of bishoprics in America. In the southern colonies where the Anglican Church was very comfortably established opposition to episcopacy was overwhelming. It was therefore only in the middle and northern colonies that there was any real call for a bishop, a plea made in the hopes that this institution would provide the basis for Anglican supremacy in these colonies. Under the circumstances it is not surprising that New England Congregationalists, New York and Pennsylvania Presbyterians and Quakers, and Maryland Catholics opposed the move vigorously.

When Thomas Secker became Archbishop of Canterbury and President of the Society for Propagating the Gospel in Foreign Parts in 1758, establishment of an American bishopric was proposed by a group of Anglican clergymen in the colonies of New Jersey and New York led by Samuel Johnson, President of King's College and father of William Samuel Johnson. In a letter congratulating the archbishop on his accession they expressed the hope that "the immediate Inspection of a Bishop . . . may be one of the Blessings of your Grace's Archiepiscopate."[2] The new archbishop was in complete sympathy with the clergymen's desires for a bishop but urged that they proceed with caution, for

what relates to Bishops, must be managed in a quiet, private Manner. Were solicitors to be sent over prematurely from America for Bishops, there would come also solicitors

assessment of Heimert's work presented by Edmund S. Morgan (*William and Mary Quarterly* XXIV, 454–459) seems persuasive in light of the work of Cross and Bridenbaugh.

[2] "Anglican clergy of New Jersey and New York" to Thomas Secker, June 22, 1758; Bernard Knollenberg, *Origin of the American Revolution, 1759–1766* (New, revised edn., New York, 1961), 83.

against them: a flame would be raised, and we should never carry our point.[3]

The Tories saw the appointment of an American bishop as a method of strengthening aristrocratic rule in the northern colonies. Cadwallader Colden very frankly stated this. The elected Assembly was a danger to a true balance in government. The only compensation would be to strengthen royal and aristocratic control, through the mediums of the governor and the Council.[4] William Eddis, a royal customs officer from Maryland, was even more specific on this point. Writing in 1770, he noted that if a nobility had been created in America and if bishoprics had been established,

It would most assuredly have greatly tended to cherish a steady adherence to monarchical principles and have more strongly riveted the attachment of the colonies to the [mother country].[5]

By 1764 many Episcopalians believed that their struggle to establish an episcopate had almost been completed. Dr. Samuel Auchmuty, a rector in New York City, was ready to carry the battle even further. Once a bishopric was established he planned to seek a Parliamentary act which would enable the Anglican minority in New York "to erect every County . . . into a parish, and make the Inhabitants pay Taxes, toward the support of a minister of the Established Church."[6] This was written just five months before the passage of the Stamp Act unified colonial opinion against the measure and those who supported it. Apart from those colonists who held royal

---

[3] Thomas Secker to Samuel Johnson, May 22, 1764; *ibid.*, 84.

[4] *Letters and Papers of Cadwallader Colden, Collections* of the New York Historical Society (New York, 1918–1923, 1934–1935), IX, 252–254.

[5] William Eddis, *Letters from America, Historical and Descriptive: Comprising Occurrences from 1769, to 1777, Inclusive* (London, 1792), 51–53.

[6] Bridenbaugh, *Mitre and Sceptre*, 246–247.

office, the one organized group to resist colonial opposition to the act was the Episcopal clergy of New England and the Middle Colonies. The Anglican clergy opposed any resistance to the Stamp Act as disloyalty to the crown. They proposed a policy of passive obedience which was resented by most Americans. As Dr. Benjamin Church was to state in 1773:

> The preacher may tell us of passive obedience, that tyrants are scourges . . . to chastise a sinful nation, and are to be submitted to . . . but men are not to be harangued out of their senses; human nature and self-preservation will eternally arm the brave and vigilant, against slavery and oppression.[7]

The policy of passive obedience linked the Anglican clergy with the hated measure in the minds of most Americans and assured that the dissenting colonists would see the establishment of episcopacy as just another step in the attempts of the British government to enslave the colonies, for many Americans believed that the bishops would interfere in politics. As one dissenter felt compelled to ask: "Is the *American* bishop to touch or affect no man's property? Is he to make no alteration in the civil condition of any of the people? On what then must he maintain his episcopal port and dignity?—On *American* air only?"[8] Believing that a bishopric, no matter how circumscribed, must infringe on religious liberty the dissenting colonists not only opposed the Stamp Act vehemently but the establishment of a bishopric as well, believing that both were part of the same plot. This became even more true for Patriots when the Townshend Acts were passed. As William Livingston of New York wrote, the increased "encroachments that have lately been made on our civil liberties" lead one to

---

[7] Speech in Boston on the occasion of the third anniversary of the Massacre, March 5, 1773; Alden T. Vaughan (ed.), *Chronicles of the American Revolution* (New York, 1965), 39–40.

[8] Quoted in Cross, *Anglican Episcopate*, 153.

believe that as Americans were being deprived of their civil liberties, England was trying to lead the colonists into "ecclesiastical bondage" as part of the "bargain."[9]

It is undoubtedly true that most dissenting clergymen opposed the introduction of bishops into the colonies at least partly for religious reasons. Many New England clergymen feared the loss of leading members of their own churches to the Anglicans. This was especially true in Connecticut where the Society for Propagating the Gospel in Foreign Parts had undertaken active proselytizing work throughout the eighteenth century. In 1722 alone several Congregational clergymen, notably Timothy Cutler, rector of Yale College, and Samuel Johnson, pastor of the West Haven Congregational Church and father of William Samuel Johnson, had converted to Anglicanism. The growth of the Church of England in the colony proceeded accordingly. From one church in 1722 the number grew to thirty-five by 1763 and to over eighty by the outbreak of the Revolution.[10]

But it was also true that most dissenters saw in the call for a bishopric a danger to political and civil liberties. John Adams wrote of this danger some years later. He claimed that the plan "spread an universal alarm against the authority of Parliament." But this was not solely ecclesiastical. Bishoprics could not be established without an act of Parliament "and if Parliament could tax us, they could establish the Church of England, with all its creeds, articles, tests, ceremonies, and tithes, and prohibit all other churches, as conventicles and schism shops."[11] Other colonists discovered the same link between taxation and episcopacy. They saw both facets of British policy as part of the same general trend. Francis Alison,

---

[9] "American Whig," *New York Gazette*, March 14, 1768.

[10] Gipson, *British Empire*, XI, 288–289. Beardsley, *Episcopal Church in Connecticut*, I, chaps. 17–22.

[11] John Adams to Hezekial Niles, February 13, 1818; Adams, *Works*, X, 288.

Vice-Provost of the College of Philadelphia, stated this most succinctly when he wrote: "Every attempt upon American liberty has always been accompanied with endeavours to settle bishops among us."[12]

It is interesting that the British government looked at the controversy in much the same way as did the dissenting colonists. During the French and Indian War calls by English and American clergymen for the establishment of a bishopric were turned down by the Pitt ministry which did not wish to antagonize the colonies by such a move. The passage of the Stamp Act and colonial opposition to it had threatened to wreck the empire as thoroughly as the war. The British government therefore had little desire to stir up non-Anglicans in the colonies over another, esssentially peripheral, issue. The political implications of bishoprics were so dangerous, in view of American opposition to Parliament, that the government was unwilling to add to the hostility Americans already felt towards British colonial policy. Therefore the British government never took any active steps towards the establishment of a bishopric. Yet, Anglican clergymen in the colonies continued to agitate for such an establishment and in the period from 1765 to 1775 the question had a great deal of political significance in the colonies both for the supporters and for the opponents of the established church.

This can be seen most clearly in the events which took place in New York during these years. For many years the Anglicans and Presbyterians in the colony had been contesting for political as well as religious control of the colony. To the Presbyterians, the scheme for an Anglican bishopric was an assertion of imperial authority which threatened political as well as religious freedom in New York.

The controversy began in the 1750's with the establishment of King's College. This event, although ecclesiastical in

---

[12] "Centenel," *Pennsylvania Journal,* July 7, 1768.

character, had a great deal of political significance which helped to color New York politics for the next twenty years. King's was to be established as an Episcopalian institution, but the dispute was not primarily a theological one and only partly ecclesiastical. The primary issues at stake were who should charter the college and whether or not the Anglican Church was established in the colony. Opposition to the Anglican establishment was directed by the New York Triumverate. *The Independent Reflector,* written primarily by William Livingston and William Smith, devoted nine papers to the issue. The quarrel ultimately led to the suppression of the *Reflector.* Smith argued that the proposed institution should be chartered by the legislature and placed under its control, in effect leaving the institution in the hands of the representatives of the people of the colony. He wrote that since the college was to be supported by public funds it should not be controlled by, or for "the ignominious Uses" of a minority of the population.[13] If this latter possibility was to be the case, Smith was convinced that "it will necessarily prove destructive to the civil and religious Rights of the People."[14] By placing the college in the hands of one religious sect, the support of others would be lost. Since King's College would cater to the children of Anglicans, within a short time a new religious and political elite would grow up in the colony. This new elite would control the colony since it is the educated who attain high public office. Therefore, the Anglican minority would come to control New York politics.[15]

William Smith proposed that the college should not cater to any particular religious group, be chartered by the legislature, and serve all the people. The personnel of the institution should be free to attend any church they so desired and "the Corporation be absolutely inhibited the making of any By-Laws relating to Religion, except such as compel them

[13] *Independent Reflector,* 182.
[14] *Ibid.,* 181.
[15] *Ibid.,* 180–181.

to attend Divine Service at some church or other, every Sabbath."[16] In order to give all deserving young men a chance to enter the college, Smith also proposed that the legislature pass an act establishing two grammar schools in each county to be supported by public funds.[17] Smith and Livingston proposed that these schools, to be supported with funds appropriated by the legislature, should be controlled by agencies acceptable to all the people and therefore be secular institutions.

Smith and Livingston, along with *The Independent Reflector,* ultimately lost the fight. King's College was established as an Episcopalian institution; *The Independent Reflector* was suppressed. But they laid the groundwork for the later struggle over the establishment of episcopacy in the Province of New York. During the conflict the colony split on religious grounds, a split accentuated by the religious beliefs of the opponents in the struggle. Lieutenant Governor DeLancey, leader of the fight for a royal charter, was an Anglican; Smith and Livingston, as well as their Assembly supporters, were Presbyterians. Thus the conflict concerning King's College was fought on two levels, levels which combined in the persons of the participants.

The names given to the two contending political factions in New York help to illustrate the importance of the religious issue in provincial affairs. The party which was led by Smith, Livingston and Scott was known by three names in the pre-revolutionary period. They were indiscriminately called the Livingston faction, the Whig Party and the Presbyterian Party; while the DeLancey faction was also called the Tory Party or the Anglican Party. That religious differences helped to delineate political ideology for the colonial New York oligarchs can be seen clearly from the writings of the Anglican clergyman Samuel Auchmuty. In 1768, when a member of the New York Council was dying, he wrote to the Bishop of

---

[16] *Ibid.,* 201
[17] *Ibid.,* 422.

London asking him to watch over the appointment to the coming vacancy,

> lest we have another Presbyterian run upon us. The whole Council (except one) belong to the Church. That one [William Smith] came in, in a Clandestine Manner; another may do the same. . . . It is a vile policy to trust avowed Republicans with posts under the British Government.[18]

To Auchmuty and the Anglicans of New York the triumvirate of Smith, Livingston and Scott were the notorious leaders of the Whig Party "which you Sir know, are Enemies to Monarchy and the established church."[19] Whiggery, republicanism and Presbyterianism in New York were linked together by the Anglican clergy who saw in the Livingston faction a threat to episcopacy and ultimately to British suzerainty over the colony. Conversely, the Whigs regarded the attempt to impose an Anglican establishment as a threat to political as well as religious rights and freedom.

The controversy over the question of a bishopric reached its peak in New York in 1767 when a sermon was preached before the Society for Propagating the Gospel in Foreign Parts which strongly suggested that an American bishopric be founded. The Presbyterians feared the coming of a bishop. The controversy over the chartering of King's College had not been forgotten and the publication of William Smith's history of New York was taken by the Anglicans to mean that a concerted attack was to be made by the Presbyterians. As Dr. Samuel Johnson complained to the Archbishop of Canterbury in 1759:

> One book indeed which has, I imagine been a principal occasion for the complaints . . . is the History of New York

---

[18] Samuel Auchmuty to the Bishop of London, July 9, 1768; Bridenbaugh, *Mitre and Sceptre*, 262.

[19] Samuel Auchmuty to Sir William Johnson, January 4, 1769; Simon Gratz Collection, Historical Society of Pennsylvania.

lately published in London, which doubtless Your Grace
has seen. This was wrote by one Smith of this Town. . .
This Smith is a lawyer here of some note, who with two
others of the same profession, Livingston and Scott, all bitter enemies to our Church and College, were believed to
be the Chief writers of the Reflector & Watch Towers—And
I believe one of the leading occassions of his writing this
history was, that he might abuse the Church.[20]

In 1768 William Livingston, with the help of William Smith
and John Morin Scott, began to publish a series of essays
under the pseudonym of "The American Whig."[21] These essays
made a strong connection between the religious issue and imperial policies. To the New York Triumvirate the issue was
just as potent as the Stamp Act or Townshend Acts had been.
As "The American Whig" wrote:

A bishop and his officers, independent of the people! I
tremble at the thought. . . . Rouse then, Americans! You
have as much to fear from such a minister of the Church
as you had lately from a minister of state.[22]

The triumvirate looked upon the bishopric controversy as
merely one phase of the overall struggle with England. The
religious question, in their minds, had been created in an
attempt to divide Americans. "Considering the encroachments that have lately been made on our civil liberties, and

[20] Samuel Johnson to Thomas Secker, March 20, 1759; *Documents
Relative to the Colonial History of the State of New York* (ed. E. B.
O'Callaghan; 15 vols., Albany, 1856–1887), VII, 371. This last assertion is unfounded and was probably based upon a perusal of the appendix to the *History* which deals with the problem of the separation
of church and state and with the Anglican claim to Church of England
establishment in New York. To this reader the account seems to be
judicious, fairly unbiased, and based wholly on problems of law and
precedent. See: Smith, *History of New York*, I, Appendix, Chapter Four,
284–295.
[21] "The American Whig," *New York Gazette*, March 14, 1768–July
24, 1769.
[22] *New York Gazette*, April 11, 1768.

that we can scarcely obtain redress against one injurious project but another is forming against us—considering the poverty and distress of the colonies by the restrictions on our trade, and how peculiarly necessary it is, in these times of common calamity, to be united amongst ourselves" it seemed preposterous to "The American Whig" that the Anglicans of New York were appealing to England for a bishop. Aside from the fact that the British government was trying to deprive the colonists of their civil liberties, American Anglicans were trying "to involve us in ecclesiastical bondage into the bargain."[23]

William Smith's own position on this question and on the whole question of religious liberty can be seen by his actions as a member of the New York Council, by an essay which he wrote in 1768, and through his *Diary*.[24] Smith's attitude on the introduction of bishops into the colonies was based on a fear of oppression. The dissenting sects were "beyond all comparison more numerous" than the Anglicans. They had left England for religious reasons, and the introduction of an episcopate would be, Smith was afraid, the forerunner of the establishment of the Church of England throughout the colonies and the loss of the religious freedom which the dissenters possessed. This would almost certainly lead to the oppression of the Protestant sects. He concluded that

It is therefore absolutely necessary that a Scheme which may be productive of the greatest Evils should be . . . opposed in all lawful Ways. . . . Mischiefs . . . will necessarily flow from the introduction of an Order of Men who once did persecute and . . . may attempt it again.[25]

In accordance with his general beliefs on religious toleration, Smith conceded the possibility of bishoprics in America

---

[23] *Ibid.*, March 14, 1768.
[24] *WS Diary* I, 42–43.
[25] *Ibid.*, 43.

if proper safeguards were provided for other religious de-
nominations. On this the greatness and peace of America
depended. Whether due to accident or because of the early
colonists' principles, the British colonies in North America
were composed of a variety of religious sects. Considering
the extent and diversity of the continent,

> it is an Article of the Utmost Importance that all Protestant
> Sects should injoy a Parity of Privileges and consequently
> that Great Britain ought never to impose any general re-
> ligious establishment upon her Colonies, but that whatever
> other Liberties are abridged they should be left free in
> Matters of Religion.[26]

Religious freedom, in Smith's view, should not be confined
to Christians, but should be extended to "Jews & any Sect
which was permitted to abide as Members of the Community."[27] In this broad based feeling of religious toleration,
Smith was careful to include even the Moslems, not that there
was any likelihood of their settling in New York.[28] Looking
at the religious state of the colonies as a whole, the New
Yorker came to the conclusion that any attempt to abridge
the religious freedom of the colonies would lead to "the Revolt of the Colonies, and that will end in the Destruction
& Ruin of the whole Empire."[29]

It is natural that William Samuel Johnson's view of the
bishopric controversy was quite different than that held by
the New York Triumvirate or than that held by his father
and other Anglican clergymen. During the years in which
the controversy reached its peak in the colonies, William
Samuel Johnson was in London as Connecticut agent. His
position with regard to a bishopric could have been a difficult

---

[26] *Ibid.*, 42.
[27] Diary entry, November 1, 1773; *ibid.*, 156–157.
[28] Diary entry, January 26, 1774; *ibid.*, 169.
[29] *Ibid.*, 42.

one. His father, Dr. Samuel Johnson, was a leading advocate of the establishment of a bishopric, while the government that William Samuel Johnson served was unalterably opposed to the establishment of episcopacy in America. That Johnson's position was not made more difficult can be attributed to the fact that although the American colonies were in an uproar about the controversy, there was little thought in English official circles of establishing an American bishopric. The only call for a bishopric had come from the Society for Propagating the Gospel in Foreign Parts and British churchmen. It had never been taken up by any of the King's ministers. From Pitt to North, Prime Ministers had no desire to stir up further opposition to the home government in the colonies. This was especially true after the Stamp Act crisis. Therefore no steps were ever taken by the British government to send a bishop to America. William Samuel Johnson, seeing that the call of the Episcopal clergy in North America was having little, if any, effect in England, advised his father to moderate his ideas so as to avoid stirring up antagonism at home.[30]

At the same time that his father was petitioning for the appointment of an American bishop, the government he served was calling on William Samuel Johnson to oppose such an appointment. There was a great deal of opposition, as we have seen, among Connecticut Congregationalists to bishops and Johnson was requested to oppose an appointment. Although he was an Anglican, he seems to have done so to the best of his ability. But at the same time he tried to calm the fears that had arisen in Connecticut. In reply to a letter by Governor Jonathan Trumbull asking what had been done regarding bishops in England, Johnson replied:

It is not intended, at present, to send any Bishops into the American colonies; had it been, I certainly should have acquainted you with it. And should it be done at all, you

---

[30] William Samuel Johnson to Samuel Johnson, June 30, 1768; Bancroft Transcripts, Connecticut Papers.

may be assured it will be done in such a manner as in no degree to prejudice, nor, if possible, even give the least offence to any denomination of Protestants. It has indeed been merely a religious, in no respects a political, scheme. . . . More than this would be thought rather disadvantageous than beneficial, and *I assure you would be opposed by no man with more zeal than myself, even as a friend to the Church of England.*[31]

William Samuel Johnson probably, like his father, would have liked to have seen a bishopric established in the colonies. He was able to avoid a conflict of interest primarily because he believed that the appointment of a bishop was unlikely for political reasons.

Yet once he had returned to Connecticut and was no longer a government spokesman, Johnson spoke out on the issue. He urged the British government to establish an episcopacy in America without waiting for the officials of an American colony to ask for one. He was sure that the Americans would never take it upon themselves to ask for a bishop because of the dissenter's fear that such an establishment would "tend to the increase of the Chh of Engd in the Colonies."[32] Johnson was a Whig, but he was also an Anglican and could not conceive of a situation in which the interests of the Church of England and the colonies could clash. Unlike the New York Presbyterians he had no fear of an Anglican tyranny in the colonies and believed that their best interests were "one and the same & that whoever best supports the one will be found most effectually to serve the other."[33] He was of course advocating the establishment of a non-political episcopacy, one in which the bishop would have solely ecclesiastical pow-

---

[31] William Samuel Johnson to Jonathan Trumbull, March 26, 1770; Beardsley, *Episcopal Church in Connecticut*, I, 265–266.

[32] William Samuel Johnson to Bishop Lowth of Oxford, October 31, 1772; William Samuel Johnson Papers, Connecticut Historical Society.

[33] William Samuel Johnson to John Pownall, May 20, 1772; *ibid.*

ers and no secular powers. He could not see how this could subvert American liberties and as an Anglican could not understand the dissenters' fears of such an establishment.

In the episcopacy conflict we find an identity of interest between the Whigs and Whig-Loyalists, although William Samuel Johnson tended towards the Anglican position. He probably did this because, being so close to the problem through his father, he saw the conflict as being purely a religious one. The opposition, Johnson believed, was of religious dissenters, motivated by religious reasons, and was not politically inspired. His father's sentiments were identical. Dr. Samuel Johnson imputed motives of religion to William Smith's opposition to the episcopacy, motives which Smith did not hold. William Smith, as a Presbyterian, did oppose the appointment of American bishops on religious grounds, but they were overshadowed by the political motives he saw in the actions of the adherents of the Church of England. To Smith the introduction of bishops into America would eventually lead to an abridgement of American rights and liberties. If the British government could establish the Anglican Church in the colonies and force all to support it, then it could also establish a despotism if it so desired. The solution to this was to maintain the general separation between church and state which existed in New York.

The quarrel between Anglicans and dissenters did not end until the outbreak of the American Revolution when it merged into the general struggle. It was the outgrowth of the independent development of the colonies for a century and a half. As long as there was nothing to call it forth, opposition to episcopacy lay dormant in America. But the Anglicans had the misfortune of petitioning for bishoprics at a time when the colonies were tending more and more towards separation from Great Britain. The decade beginning 1765 saw the British government make a great many encroachments upon what the American colonists considered to be their rights. They were not in a position, nor did they have the inclination, to accept any innovation that menaced their liberties.

To the British government the question of an American bishopric died with the events occasioning the Stamp Act. Realizing the political implications of bishops to Americans, the ministry had no desire to present the colonists with another inflammatory issue. However the Anglican clergy of the northern colonies continued to agitate. Dissenters and Whigs saw in the clergy a group of men in whom loyalty to their church and therefore the Crown transcended American rights and local loyalties. They were therefore suspected of disloyalty and their ideas were considered subversive. The fact was not lost on the Patriots that the clergy entertained political motives in advocating episcopacy. As William Sweet has pointed out, the loyalty of Anglicans to Great Britain was directly related to their strength in each colony. In those colonies where Anglicanism was strongest (i.e. Virginia) the smallest proportion of episcopal advocates were to be found.[34] But perhaps of more consequence was the fact that from the strength of their petitions the Anglican clergy aroused the fear that the British government was supporting the establishment of episcopacy in America. We now know that there was no governmental support and that American fears were imaginary. But what is more important is that many colonists suspected that government support for the project did exist and this suspicion had a great deal of influence in alienating the colonies from Great Britain. Hence the bishopric controversy was one of a number of causes which tended to accentuate the growing split between Great Britain and the American colonies.

There can be no doubt that the dissenting colonists treated the struggle over a bishopric as being politically inspired, for the situation changed drastically after the Revolution. No

[34] William W. Sweet, *Religion in the Development of American Culture* (New York, 1952), 14.

longer was the introduction of bishops opposed by the Patriots. John Adams wrote of the situation some years later.

> Where is the man to be found at this day, when we see Methodistical bishops, bishops of the Church of England, and bishops, archbishops, and Jesuits of the church of Rome, with indifference, who will believe that the apprehension of Episcopacy contributed fifty years ago, as much as any other cause, to arouse the attention, not only of the inquiring mind, but of the common people, and urge them to close thinking on the constitutional authority of parliament over the colonies? This, nevertheless, was a fact as certain as any in the history of North America. The objection was not merely to the office of a bishop, even though that was dreaded, but to the authority of parliament, on which it must be founded.[35]

Adams may have overstated the impact which this issue had in causing the American Revolution, but the reasons he advanced about the cause of the issue cannot be denied. That it was politically inspired is beyond doubt. The Tories as well as the Whigs had a political motive in this conflict. Anglicans such as Colden and Eddis saw in the episcopacy a means of strengthening royal government and control in America. Most Whigs saw the issue as one facet of the main issue at stake— the ability of Parliament to legislate for the colonies. If Parliament could legislate for the colonies on religious matters, then it could do so on matters of taxation. The issue at stake was whether or not Parliament could legitimately legislate the internal affairs of the colonies. It was not difficult for men such as William Smith, John Adams and William Livingston to decide that if Parliament could not tax the colonies, it also could not legislate for the colonies in religious, or any other matters.

---

[35] John Adams to J. Morse, December 2, 1815; Adams, *Works*, X, 185.

5

THE ROAD TO CIVIL WAR

The quiet interlude which began with the collapse of non-importation was ended on the night of June 9, 1772, when the customs schooner *Gaspee* was attacked and burned by eight boatloads of men from Providence, Rhode Island.[1] The incident itself was relatively unimportant, yet it marked the beginning of the second phase of the struggle between Great Britain and America, concerning the rights and privileges of the colonies, which culminated in revolution and civil war in America. During the period immediately before the outbreak of the Revolution many crises occurred which hastened the coming of civil war to America. Whig-Loyalist response to these events varied according to the individual. During the period they did not behave in a unified fashion. Because of their responses to the Tea Parties, the Coercive Acts and Lexington-Concord they either gained, lost or maintained their political influence within the Whig hierarchy. It was during this period that Robert Alexander, Andrew Allen, Dr. Benjamin Church and Peter Van Schaack came to the fore, while

---

[1] I have been unable to ascertain the views of any of the Whig-Loyalists about this event. William Smith wrote a letter to a Mr. Woolridge on January 2, 1773 outlining his views on the *Gaspee* but I have been unable to locate this letter. See: Diary entry, January 4, 1773; *WS Diary* I, 136.

Daniel Dulany, William Samuel Johnson and Daniel Leonard began to lose their influence and power.

The burning of the *Gaspee* was followed by an announcement by Governor Hutchinson of Massachusetts that henceforth his salary would be paid by the Crown. Massachusetts, followed by other colonies, began to organize new Committees of Correspondence, for the Whigs viewed this action as a new attempt to tighten royal control in the colonies. In 1774 John Hancock, in a speech written by Benjamin Church and Joseph Warren, stated this clearly:

> The British ministry have annexed a salary to the office of the governor of this province, to be paid out of a revenue, raised in America without our consent. They have attempted to render our courts of justice the instruments of extending the authority of acts of the British Parliament over this colony, by making the judges dependent on the British administration for their support. But this people will never be enslaved with their eyes open.[2]

When Parliament passed the Tea Act on May 10, 1773, the colonials were already organized. The decision of the East India Company to send tea to America found the smugglers and merchants who would be undersold by the company in an apparent alliance with the Sons of Liberty. "A new flame," William Smith wrote, "is apparently kindling in America." He saw in the Tea Act a threat to domestic political parties, believing that they would be "swallowed up in the general Opposition to the Parliamentary Project of raising the Arm of Government by Revenue Laws—"[3] As had been the case

[2] Address by John Hancock to the people of Boston on the fourth anniversary of the Boston Massacre, March 5, 1774; Vaughan, *Chronicles of the American Revolution*, 79.

[3] Diary entry, October 13, 1773; *WS Diary* I, 156. This in some measure displeased William Smith as he believed that, in some respects, New York was unique and had unique problems as well as disputes with other colonies.

in previous years, Smith was again approached by the radicals
for advice, this time by the Committee of Correspondence led
by Philip Livingston, Isaac Low, Isaac Sears and Alexander
MacDougall. They wanted Smith to intercede with the Council and present their views to the governor. Although most
New Yorkers apparently approved of Governor Tryon's plan
to land and store the tea that the East India Company shipped
to New York, the committee did not want it to be landed.
They stated, through William Smith, "that if it was suffered
to remain on Ship board they would guard it safely."[4]

William Smith's first disagreement with the radicals came
at this time. As a member of the New York Council and
closely identified with the Establishment he could see Governor Tryon's predicament as well as the viewpoint of the
Sons of Liberty. He believed that allowances should be made
for the governor, who was returning to England "& wished
to be able to hold up his Head at Court, & before his Countrymen." Smith did not want to block the landing of the tea
on the wharf, for such an action might lead to bloodshed.
He addressed the radicals in this fashion, not because he disapproved of their attempts to stop the tea from being landed,
but "to intimate the Danger arising from the Gov'rs Spirit in
this business, & that they pushed him too hard." He was
concerned primarily with preventing the shedding of blood
over the issue. Apparently Livingston and Low approved of
Smith's sentiments, but Sears and MacDougall remained fixed
in their purpose. MacDougall even asked the question: "What
if we prevent the Landing, & kill Govr. & all the Council?"
This hypothetical query startled not only William Smith, but
Philip Livingston as well.[5] Smith's advice at the time apparently did not alienate MacDougall and Sears to any great
degree, for Smith consulted with them about further action
to be taken with regard to tea shipments on the evening of

---

[4] Diary entry, December 1, 1773; *ibid.*, 157–158.
[5] Diary entry, December 13, 1773; *ibid.*, 158.

December 18th.⁶ The situation was this: Governor Tryon desired to allow the tea to land, the committee wanted to send it back to England, and William Smith attempted to moderate by compromise. He wanted the Sons of Liberty to allow the tea to be landed, placed in storage, but not sold.

At this point, wrote William Smith, "The Boston News astonished the Town—Those who were for storing the Tea now affect to change Sentiments."⁷ This number included William Smith, who came around to the view that storing the tea in New York would help neither the East India Company nor the crown.⁸ He therefore advised returning the tea to England. Smith was approached, in his capacity as an attorney, by three New York merchants who were acting as agents for the East India Company to write a letter for them to be sent to the captain of the tea ship when it arrived in New York harbor. Smith readily consented and the letter, in Smith's hand—but signed by Henry White, Abraham Lott and Benjamin Booth—is an exposition of Smith's views and opinions at the time.⁹ The agents apparently agreed to this critique of the Tea Act for several reasons. Aside from the intimidation and threats they received from the Sons of Liberty, they were New York merchants with mercantile establishments. To these men more was at stake than just the East India Company tea; their private businesses were involved as well. A letter by William Smith could aid their precarious positions with regard to the Sons of Liberty. In the letter the Tea Act was considered to be

Proof of a Confederacy between Administration and the Company to give Efficacy to the Project of establishing a

---

⁶ Diary entry, December 18, 1773; *ibid.,* 162.

⁷ Diary entry, December 22, 1773; *ibid.,* 163. Dr. Benjamin Church was one of the leaders of the Tea Party; *Appleton's Cyclopaedia of American Biography,* I, 612.

⁸ Diary entry, December 25, 1773; *WS Diary* I, 165.

⁹ Letter of December 29, 1773; *ibid.,* 165–166.

Revenue for the Support of a Government in this Country totally independent of us & yet maintained at our Expense, and [we have] adopted an Opinion that such an Establishment will plunge [the colonies] into a most abject Slavery.

William Smith's reaction to the Tea Act and to the Boston Tea Party was one of moderation. He did not approve of the tea monopoly, nor did he want to see company tea sold in America, yet he was not willing to see the property of others destroyed to prevent this from happening. He proposed that the tea be stored until such time as a decision on the matter should be made in England. After the Bostonians had acted, William Smith believed that the tea being shipped to New York should not be allowed to land lest it be destroyed in the same manner. This stand was in conflict with the opinions of both Whigs and Tories. To Governor Thomas Hutchinson the "barbarous" tea party was the boldest stroke to date by the popular leaders to gain independence. He was sure that with this action they hoped to involve the people to such an extent that they could not turn back.[10] In retrospect, Joseph Galloway took a similar view. However he imputed the cause of the opposition to the Tea Act to the instigation of the smugglers and merchants who would lose their livelihood. The American people, he believed, would gain because the new selling price of tea would be one-half of the previous price.[11] All of the above opinions may be contrasted with that of John Adams who wrote that the Boston Tea Party was "the most magnificent movement of all. There is a dignity, a majesty, a sublimity, in this last effort of the patriots, that I greatly admire."[12]

---

[10] Thomas Hutchinson, *The History of the Province of Massachusetts Bay* (ed. John Hutchinson; 3 vols., London, 1828), III, 312. Also see. Thomas Hutchinson to Israel Williams, December 23, 1773; Hosmer, *Thomas Hutchinson*, 303–304.

[11] Joseph Galloway, *Historical and Political Reflections on the Rise and Progress of the American Rebellion* (London, 1780), 17–18.

[12] Diary entry, December 17, 1773; Adams, *Works*, II, 323.

It was during the conflict over the Tea Act that Daniel
Leonard of Massachusetts began to tend towards Loyalism.
Until 1774, Leonard enjoyed a large degree of popularity in
Massachusetts. A graduate of the Harvard class of 1760, he
became an ardent Whig. Taunton, where he practiced law,
elected him to the Massachusetts House of Representatives
in 1770, 1771, 1773 and 1774. He was also a lieutenant colonel
in the Third Bristol County Regiment of militia. During the
period before 1774 he "had been," in John Adams's words,
"as ardent and explicit a patriot as I was."[13] In June, 1769
he voted with the Whigs to request the recall of Governor
Bernard and in 1770 was a member of a committee which
was to draw up a remonstrance to Governor Hutchinson not
to move the legislature from Boston.[14] Other members of
this committee were James Bowdoin, Dr. Benjamin Church,
Samuel Adams and John Hancock. Late in 1773 Leonard
helped to draft a letter to the king requesting the removal of
Hutchinson and Chief Justice Peter Oliver.[15] In May of the
same year the people of Taunton elected Daniel Leonard
to the Committee of Correspondence where he served with
Hancock, Samuel Adams, Dr. Benjamin Church and Elbridge
Gerry among others. Yet on February 11, 1774, Daniel
Leonard voted against the impeachment of Chief Justice
Oliver.[16] This stand for the first time brought Leonard into
direct conflict with the Patriots.

John Adams believed that the reasons for this sudden switch
were economic in origin. Leonard was a dandy and considered to be one of the "Young Bloods" of Massachusetts.

He wore a broad gold lace round the brim of his hat, he
had made his cloak glitter with laces still broader, he had
set up his chariot and pair, and constantly travelled in it

[13] John Adams to William Tudor, November 16, 1816; *ibid.*, X, 231.
[14] Ralph Davol, *Two Men of Taunton. In the Course of Human Events
1731–1829* (Taunton, Massachusetts, 1912), 225.
[15] *Ibid.*, 228.
[16] *Ibid.*, 229.

from Taunton to Boston. This made the world stare; it was a novelty. Not another lawyer in the province, attorney or barrister, of whatever age, reputation, rank or station presumed to ride in a coach or a chariot.[17]

According to Adams, Thomas Hutchinson soon perceived "that wealth and power must have charms to a heart that delighted in so much finery, and indulged in such unusual expense." His vanity was therefore courted by the Tories and he was persuaded by the governor to support the court party.[18] Adams' interpretation of Leonard's defection from the patriotic cause was widely held by Bostonians. In her satirical play The Group Mercy Otis Warren put this explanation into the mouth of Beau Trumps who is a satirical character delineation of Daniel Leonard.

> When first I enter'd on the public stage
> My country groan'd beneath base Brundo's hand,
> Virtue look'd fair and beckon'd to her lure
> Thro' truth's bright mirror I beheld her charms
> And wish'd to tread the patriotic path.
> And wear the Laurels that adorn his fame;
> I walk'd a while and tasted solid peace. . . .
> But 'twas a poor unprofitable path
> Nought to be gain'd save solid peace of mind,
> No pensions, place or title I found;
> I saw Rapatio's arts had struck so deep
> And giv'n his country such a fatal wound
> None but its foes promotion could expect;
> I trim'd, and pimp'd, and veer'd, and wav'ring stood
> But half resolv'd to show myself a knave,
> Till the Arch Traitor [Hutchinson] prowling round for aid
> Saw my suspense and bid me doubt no more;—
> He gently bow'd, and smiling took my hand,
> And whispering softly in my listening ear,

---

[17] John Adams to Dr. J. Morse, December 22, 1815; Adams, Works, X, 194–195.
[18] Ibid.

Shew'd me my name among his chosen band,
And laugh'd at virtue dignify'd by fools,
Clear'd all my doubts, and bid me persevere
In spite of the restraints, or hourly checks
Of wounded friendship, and a goaded mind,
Of all the sacred ties of truth and honour.[19]

Although he had voted with the Tories on the matter of
Oliver's impeachment, Leonard did not immediately lose his
popularity with the citizenry of Taunton. In May, 1774 he
was elected to the House of Representatives for the fifth time,
and in June was elected to the Committee of Nine of the
General Court. This committee, with Samuel Adams as chairman, was ostensibly formed to consider the general state of
affairs of the province. In reality it was to select the Massachusetts delegates to the Continental Congress. The Patriots
on the committee did not fully trust Daniel Leonard, despite
his popularity, and feared that if he knew of their plans he
would report them to General Thomas Gage. Fearing a dissolution of the General Court they avoided the discussion of
secret and controversial matters in Leonard's presence. Leonard's friend and colleague, Robert Treat Paine, who also represented Taunton in the House of Representatives, was used
to lure Daniel Leonard away from committee meetings when
the Congress was to be discussed. When the time for the
crucial vote on the election of delegates came up, Paine convinced Leonard to return to Taunton with him to attend the
county court session.[20] Since he was absent from the House
of Representatives when the issue came to a vote, Daniel
Leonard's final break with the Patriots was postponed.

The Massachusetts Government Act of May 20, 1774, virtually annulled the Massachusetts charter. Among other provisions, members of the Council, who had been elected by

---

[19] Warren, *The Group,* 8–9.
[20] Robert Treat Paine on Daniel Leonard, June, 1774; Robert Treat
Paine Papers, Massachusetts Historical Society.

the House of Representatives, were to be appointed by the
king and hold office at royal pleasure. Daniel Leonard's final
split with the Patriots came during the summer of 1774 when
he was appointed one of these Mandamus Councellors. He
was pressed by his Patriot friends to decline the post, but he
accepted the appointment. His neighbors in Taunton "in order
to express the disquietude of their minds on hearing the alarm-
ing news" forced him to flee to the protection afforded by the
British troops in Boston.[21] He remained in Boston until the
evacuation of the British Army in March, 1776.

Although John Adams attributed Leonard's defection to
the Loyalist cause to his love of luxury, other more important
reasons for his ideological reversal are evident in a series of
seventeen letters which he wrote and published in the *Massachusetts Gazette* beginning on December 12, 1774 and signed
"Massachusettensis." These letters were answered by John
Adams writing as "Novanglus."[22] In the series Daniel Leonard presented his political philosophy and described the differences between the Whig and Tory viewpoints.

The tories were for closing the controversy with Great
Britain [in 1771 after the partial repeal of the Townshend
Acts], the whigs for continuing it; the tories were for restoring government in the province, which had become
greatly relaxed by these convulsions, to its former tone;
the whigs were averse to it. . . . However, the whigs had
great advantages in the unequal contest; their scheme flat-
tered the people with the idea of independence; the tories'

---

[21] Extract of a letter from Taunton, Massachusetts, August 24, 1774;
*American Archives: Fourth Series Concerning a Documentary History of
the English Colonies in North America, from the King's Message to
Parliament, of March 7, 1774, to the Declaration of Independence by
the United States* (ed. Peter Force; 6 vols., Washington, 1837–1846), I,
732. Hereafter cited as *4: Amer. Arch.*

[22] Published together as: *Novanglus and Massachusettensis* (Boston,
1819). At the time Adams believed that "Massachusettensis" had been
written by Jonathan Sewall.

plan supposed a degree of subordination, which is rather a humiliating idea.[23]

This is not to say that Leonard ideologically was a Tory. He did, at the time, accept the label. But using the terminology of this study he was not a Tory in the sense that Thomas Hutchinson, Joseph Galloway or Jared Ingersoll were. These men had supported the Stamp Act and the Townshend Acts, Leonard had opposed them. Until 1774 he had been a Whig and a Patriot.

Part of the reason for his switch from Whiggery to Loyalism was the fact that Daniel Leonard was something of a pessimist and had an aversion to armed rebellion that overrode his fear of Great Britain. For Leonard, rebellion was "the most atrocious offense that can be perpetrated by man. . . It dissolves the social band, annihilates the security resulting from law and government, introduces fraud, violence, rapine, murder, sacrilege, and the long train of evils that riot uncontrolled in a state of nature." Besides, he was sure that the military power of Great Britain would be able to crush any rebellion in New England. Massachusetts would find that the middle and southern colonies would not support her in a war with England.[24] He also dreaded the thought that the American trade and coastline would lose the protection of the Royal Navy if independence became a reality. Without this protection American ships would be attacked and her ports would be pillaged by Spain and France. The connection with Britain had to be maintained to prevent other nations from overwhelming America.[25] Underlying these thoughts was Leonard's basic position on taxation. He maintained the

---

[23] Letter of December 19, 1774; *ibid.*, 149.

[24] Written in 1775. Quoted in Bernard Bailyn, *The Ideological Origins of the American Revolution* (Cambridge, Massachusetts, 1967), 314. Letter of December 12, 1774; *Novanglus and Massachusettensis*, 141–146.

[25] Letter of January 30, 1775; *Novanglus and Massachusettensis*, 184.

idea of the separation of internal and external taxation which had been discarded by other Whigs in the 1760's. Leonard was opposed to internal taxation. He, as of 1775, still believed that the Stamp Act had been unconstitutional. But he did believe that Parliament had the constitutional right to levy external taxes and enforce the Tea Act.[26] This was a view that brought him into ideological opposition to the Whigs.

Because political matters came to a head and the split between Patriots and Tories became more evident at an earlier date in Massachusetts, Daniel Leonard was forced to make a decision on these matters before the other Whigs under discussion were compelled to do so. Therefore, Daniel Leonard was the first of these Whigs to become a Loyalist. The Boston Tea Party seems to have influenced him greatly. He deplored the actions of the mob and believed that Great Britain had been justified in passing the Tea Act.[27] It was soon after this event that Daniel Leonard began to break away from the Patriots and allow himself to be swayed by Thomas Hutchinson.

Daniel Leonard, as "Massachusettensis," argued his position so effectively that John Adams believed himself compelled to reply. The published exchange of letters has become a classic American political dialogue. But Leonard was not writing from a true Tory position. As a Loyalist he could defend American opposition to internal taxation and he had supported the Stamp Act agitation. But he could see no valid constitutional reason to deny Britain the right of external taxation or the control of American trade. The Boston Tea Party was an inexcusably provocative act on the part of the Patriots and was being justly punished by Parliament. Thus, Daniel Leonard did not ideologically become a Tory, but occupied something of a middle position between Whig and Tory. He became, in fact, a conservative Whig-Loyalist.

26 Letter of February 27, 1775; *ibid.*, 202–203.
27 Letter of January 2, 1775; *ibid.*, 159.

The tea disorders caused Parliament to pass the Boston Port Act, the Administration of Justice Act, and the Massachusetts Government Act. These "coercive" measures were intended to punish Massachusetts for the Tea Party in particular, and for her general leadership of the colonial opposition to Great Britain. Reaction to the Coercive Acts by the various colonies was immediate. Soon after the news of the Boston Port Bill reached Baltimore, a Committee of Correspondence was established to make contact with similar groups in other colonies. Robert Alexander, the lawyer, was the first man to be appointed to it.[28] On May 31, 1774, a general meeting held at Baltimore adopted a series of resolutions urging the unity of the colonies to secure the repeal of the Port Act. They resolved that "the town of *Boston* is now suffering in the common cause of America." The means which they resolved to use to force the repeal of the obnoxious measure was to form "an Association with the several counties in this Province, and the principle [*sic*] Colonies in *America,* to put a stop to the imports from *Great Britain* . . . until the said Act shall be repealed." The Baltimore meeting also called for a "Congress of Deputies" to be held at Annapolis in order to unite the colony and to appoint delegates to a general congress of the colonies, if one was convened. Robert Alexander and nine others were appointed to the Provincial Congress and became a new Committee of Correspondence.[29] Alexander's work at the meeting must have been of importance, for the Grand Inquest for Baltimore County wrote to him

as sincere Lovers of their Country, to express in this manner, their highest Approbation of your spirited and patriotic Conduct manifested on Tuesday last in behalf of the much injured Americans; and, as a small Testimony of their Grati-

---

[28] Johnson, *Robert Alexander,* 38.
[29] Baltimore County Resolutions, May 31, 1774; *4: Amer. Arch.,* I, 366–367.

tude, to render you their Thanks for your Efforts in a Cause
in which every Subject of British America is equally and
deeply interested.[30]

Daniel Dulany was in almost complete agreement with the
Baltimore resolves. He was present at a similar meeting held
at Annapolis a few days before the Baltimore meeting and
voted against only one of the resolutions which stated "that
no lawyer should bring any action for any merchant in *Great
Britain* against an inhabitant till this Act be repealed." Dulany
opposed this measure because he believed that a discrimina-
tory loss of due process would "give a handle to our enemies
to hurt the general cause. I would have agreed to it if it had
extended to merchants in this country as well as foreign merchants." He went on to write:

> Every just, indeed every efficient measure, should be taken
> against the *British* Parliament in their designs to tax *Amer-
> ica*; for I am convinced that if once the principle of taxing
> were established, property here would not be worth hold-
> ing. But, at the same time, let us never give them an oppor-
> tunity, by our resolves, to accuse us of injustice.[31]

Daniel Dulany, ever the legalist, thereby advised a new boycott of British trade but dreaded the consequences. He opposed the measure forbidding the bringing of law suits for
British merchants on grounds of legal morality, although the
alternative he proposed would have vitiated the whole scheme.
The proposal was designed to penalize British merchants for
the actions of Parliament. This would, as would non-importa-

---

[30] John Deaver, Foreman, to Robert Alexander, June 2, 1774; *Maryland Journal and the Baltimore Advertiser*, June 4, 1774. Alexander's
biographer, Janet B. Johnson, also quotes this letter but attributes it to
Alexander's skillful handling of a law case (page 36). I think it is obvious
that the letter refers to the Baltimore meeting of May 31 which was the
previous Tuesday.

[31] Daniel Dulany to Arthur Lee, May, 1774; *4: Amer. Arch.*, I, 354–
355.

tion, put pressure on the merchants to force the repeal of
the Coercive Acts. Dulany's plan, although legally and morally
above reproach, would, by extending the boycott to American merchants as well, have brought business in America to
a halt. He was content therefore to play a passive role in the
quarrel with the mother country because of what he considered to be the illegality, not only of the Parliamentary measures, but of the colonial boycott as well.

In New York, as in Maryland, leadership of the opposition
to the Coercive Acts was vested in a committee—the Committee of Fifty which was to serve as a committee of correspondence as well. Peter Van Schaack was elected to membership in it on May 16, 1774.[32] On May 23rd, Van Schaack,
James Duane and John Jay were appointed a committee to
draw up a set of rules for the Committee of Fifty.[33] The
New York Committee of Correspondence was larger than
those of most of the colonies, a situation that William Smith
ascribed to the fact that "Many people of Property dread the
Violence of the lower Sort" and therefore sought a larger body
made up of at least some men of property.[34] Smith favored
this large committee, for as he told Alexander MacDougall, to
the British "we should appear to be united." Besides, "as the
Times grew Warm, the disaffected [Tories] would sneak from
the Committee."[35] William Smith was not a member of this
nor any other revolutionary committee, but served as an un-
official adviser to such outspoken radicals as his partner John
Morin Scott and Alexander MacDougall. As a member of the
New York Council, Smith was an official of the royal government. To take a prominent part in the extra-legal activities
of the Committee of Correspondence would have meant the
loss of his influence as a royal officeholder. As a member of

---

[32] *Ibid.*, 293.
[33] *Ibid.*, 295–296.
[34] Diary entry, May 18, 1774; *WS Diary* I, 186.
[35] Diary entry, May 20, 1774; *ibid.*, 187.

the Council Smith was in a position from which he could both influence the government and advise the radicals.

Peter Van Schaack, as a leading member of the Committee of Fifty, was prepared for war with Great Britain as early as February, 1774. Before the passage of the Boston Port Bill he believed that "the Opposition of the Colonies is growing so powerful with their increasing Strength that I believe the Parliament will begin to think conciliatory Methods the most eligible." He considered the idea of uniting American rights with a subordination to the British Parliament to be absurd and believed that "Claims so incompatible cannot be reconciled—On one side or other they must be false. God forbid the *major vis* should be necessary to decide the contest."[36] On hearing of the Boston Port Bill he wrote that "an Appeal to the Sword . . . is inevitable," believing that the colonies would never recede from "an absolute Exemption from Parliamentary Taxation in every Respect whatever." This was not only their right, but without it they did not "enjoy the Privileges of British subjects. That it *is* their Right is a Conception we cannot expect from England until Necessity should compel them to it."[37]

Although the Committee of Fifty as a whole busied itself with raising funds for the relief of the poor of Boston, there was a subcommittee to which Peter Van Schaack belonged. Its main purpose was to serve as the actual committee of correspondence and to enforce the non-importation agreement which had been agreed upon by the Committee of Fifty.[38] Peter Van Schaack was also a member of a four-man committee to request the "Importers of Goods" to meet "in order to consider the most effectual ways for stopping this growing evil."[39] He was even willing to go one step further and, in a letter, advocated a policy

---

[36] Peter Van Schaack to John Vargill, February 19, 1774; Peter Van Schaack Papers, Columbia University Library.

[37] Peter Van Schaack to John Vargill, May 13, 1774; *ibid.*

[38] *4: Amer. Arch.*, 1, 322.

[39] *Ibid.*, 328.

of non-exportation to Great Britain and the West Indies.[40] This policy was not adopted by the New York committee at the time.

William Smith was not in favor of non-importation and advised MacDougall against pushing for such an agreement "because it would be impossible to hold the Merchants to it long enough to give it the desired Effects."[41] He feared that if the agreement failed, New York would appear to be weak in British eyes. The committee was to find that William Smith was correct. They had a great deal of trouble holding the merchants in line. Where Peter Van Schaack believed that the American colonists were strong enough to attempt anything against Great Britain, William Smith realized that, in New York at least where there was a strong well organized Tory faction, serious internal differences existed that prevented New York from presenting a strong united front. Smith believed that the only hope New York had was in not attempting any act which would expose this internal dissension. He feared that non-importation would do this and urged MacDougall and the Sons of Liberty to call for a congress of all the colonies instead. He believed that Great Britain "would dread more from Congress, than from a Non-Importation, & imagine that perhaps we were preparing to call in a foreign Power."[42]

The call for a Continental Congress, which Smith echoed, was also heard in Boston. On March 5, 1774, John Hancock, in a speech written for him by Benjamin Church and Joseph Warren, urged the colonists to unite "and strengthen the hands of each other." He continued:

Permit me here to suggest a general congress of deputies, from the several houses of assembly, on the continent, as the

---

[40] Peter Van Schaack to Peter Silvester, May 21, 1774; Van Schaack, *Peter Van Schaack*, 16–17.

[41] Diary entry, May 20, 1774; *WS Diary* I, 187.

[42] Diary entry, May 18, 1774; *ibid.*, 186.

most effectual method of establishing such a union. . . . At
such a Congress a firm foundation may be laid for the security of our rights and liberties, a system may be formed for our
common safety, by a strict adherence to which, we shall be
able to frustrate any attempts to overthrow our constitution;
restore peace and harmony to America, and . . . free ourselves
from those unmannerly pillagers who impudently tell us, that
they are licensed by an act of the British parliament to thrust
their dirty hands into the pockets of every American.[43]

Dr. Church, as a member of the Sons of Liberty, was also called
upon to serve on the committee protesting the passage of the
Port Act.

Although most of the Whig-Loyalists were in favor of a congress, only two were elected to represent their colonies, and
they refused to attend. Daniel Dulany was asked informally by
members of the Maryland Convention if he would serve, but
he refused. He believed, however, that "a petition & remonstrance from the Congress to the King & Parliament was the
properest mode of proceeding in order to obtain redress."[44] On
July 13, 1774, the Committee of Correspondence for the colony
of Connecticut nominated Eliphalet Dyer, William Samuel
Johnson, Erastus Wolcott, Silas Deane and Richard Law, or any
three of them, to represent Connecticut in the congress in order
to "advise on proper measures to promote the general good and
welfare of the whole, and for obtaining a redress of the grievances under which we labour."[45] Of the five men selected, only
Eliphalet Dyer and Silas Deane accepted the appointment. The
others, including Johnson, declined.[46] Johnson had participated
in the deliberations of the Stamp Act Congress and as late as
October, 1769 wrote in favor "of the firm universal union of all
the people of America, to assert and maintain their indubitable

---

[43] Vaughan, *Chronicles of the American Revolution,* 80.
[44] Land, *Dulanys of Maryland,* 312.
[45] *4: Amer. Arch.,* I, 554.
[46] *Ibid.,* 895.

rights."[47] But by the time of the first Continental Congress he disapproved of the idea of a congress and wrote to his friend Richard Jackson that he was resolved to "do everything possible to keep the Ardour of my Countrymen within Bounds, tho' it is more than possible I shall forfeit their esteem."[48] Johnson's actions should be contrasted with those of Jared Ingersoll or Joseph Galloway. Although Johnson disapproved of the Congress and refused to serve in it, he did nothing to hinder those who believed in it. Ingersoll put forth all his efforts to dissuade New York, Connecticut and Pennsylvania from sending delegates to what he considered to be an illegal body.[49] Galloway, on the other hand, attended in hopes of being able to control the Congress.

In New York the call for the election of delegates to the Continental Congress was taken up by the Committee of Fifty which had, since its inception, taken on a conservative hue. When, on July 19th the committee called a meeting to choose the New York delegates and, as William Smith put it, to "approve certain pusillanimous Resolves," John Morin Scott and the radicals forced the rejection of the conservative resolves and delegates.[50] William Smith fervently hoped that the Congress would develop into an annual parliament, "the grand Wittenagemott," as he proudly called it, and was highly disappointed when it appeared as if New York was, due to the split between conservatives and radicals, going to be the last colony to appoint delegates.[51] It is probable that Peter Van Schaack agreed with William Smith on this issue. As he wrote in a letter to the Connecticut Committee of Correspondence on July 11, 1774: "The sentiments . . . of the necessity of a Congress,

---

[47] William Samuel Johnson to William Pitkin, October 16, 1769; Bancroft Transcripts, William Samuel Johnson Correspondence.
[48] William Samuel Johnson to Richard Jackson, August 30, 1774; *ibid.*
[49] Gipson, *Ingersoll*, 329.
[50] Diary entry, July 20, 1774; *WS Diary* I, 189.
[51] William Smith to Philip Schuyler, July 23, 1774; Schuyler Papers, New York Public Library.

are supported with such reasons as must command the assent
of every well wisher to the rights and privileges of America."[52]
During the deliberations of the Congress, Van Schaack hoped
that all political activity would be suspended so as to give the
delegates the opportunity to use their collective abilities to the
utmost. This was necessary, he wrote to James Duane, one of
the New York delegates, because private judgments should
"submit to the united Sense of the collective body."[53]

The first Continental Congress, which met from September
5 to October 26, 1774, not only sent the petitions to the king and
Parliament which Daniel Dulany had called for, but also promulgated the Continental Association. This association constituted a pledge by the delegates that their colonies would
institute non-importation, non-consumption and non-exportation of all goods to and from Great Britain. It also instituted
extra-legal committees to be elected in each colony to enforce
the association.[54] As was the case with William Samuel Johnson,
Daniel Dulany refused to serve in Congress but did approve
of its deliberations up to a point. He agreed with Congress
when it petitioned the king and Parliament for a redress of
grievances, but when the Continental Association was decreed,
Dulany drew the line. He still believed that what he believed
to be illegal measures could not be used to combat unconstitutional acts of Parliament.[55]

Robert Alexander, Dr. Benjamin Church, Peter Van Schaack
and William Smith supported the resolves of the first Continental Congress and helped to implement the Continental
Association in their respective colonies. On November 12, 1774,
the Baltimore County Committee of Observation and a new
Baltimore Committee of Correspondence were elected. Robert

---

[52] 4: Amer. Arch., I, 305.

[53] Draft of letter, Peter Van Schaack to James Duane, 1774; Peter Van
Schaack Papers, Columbia University Library.

[54] English Historical Documents; Volume IX: American Colonial Documents to 1776 (ed. Merrill Jensen; London, 1955), 813–816.

[55] Land, Dulanys of Maryland, 312.

Alexander served as clerk for the election and was elected to both committees, placing second in the poll for the twenty-nine members of the Committee of Observation and first in the poll for members of the Committee of Correspondence.[56] The function of the Committee of Observation was to seek out persons not abiding by the Continental Association. Alexander must have served the committee well, for on January 16, 1775, he was elected to the next provincial convention as one of Baltimore's delegates and on March 6, 1775, was elected Secretary of the Committee of Observation.[57]

In Massachusetts, the House of Representatives, in defiance of General Gage, reconstituted itself as a Provincial Congress. A Committee of Safety was established with power to call out the militia and purchase armaments. Dr. Benjamin Church, an active member of the Sons of Liberty for many years, was immediately elected to the Provincial Congress along with Dr. Joseph Warren and Nathaniel Appleton by the Boston Town Meeting. They were instructed "to act upon such Matters . . . most likely to preserve the Liberties of all America."[58] Church and Warren had previously constituted a subcommittee of the Boston Committee of Correspondence which was charged with drawing up a circular letter proposing a "Solemn League and Covenant" not to import, export or consume British goods.[59] Soon after his election to the Provincial Congress, Church, along with John Hancock and Joseph Warren, was appointed to the Committee of Safety. During the ensuing year he alternated with Hancock as chairman of the committee.[60] At the time Dr. Church was apparently more radical than James Otis. At a Boston Town Meeting held on November 3, 1774, Otis tried to calm the passions of the mob, but Church was incendi-

---

[56] 4: Amer. Arch., I, 975. Maryland Journal, November 30, 1774.
[57] Johnson, Robert Alexander, 45–47.
[58] Gipson, British Empire, XII, 161.
[59] Ibid., 150–151.
[60] Ibid., 162. French, General Gage's Informers, 118, 148.

ary and attempted to incite the citizens of Boston to action against the British.[61]

In New York the Committee of Fifty dissolved itself and was replaced by a new agency, the Committee of Sixty, formed to implement the Continental Association. As a known friend to non-importation and non-consumption, Peter Van Schaack was unanimously elected to the new committee. He was one of twenty-nine members of the Committee of Fifty to find a place in the Committee of Sixty.[62] This election constituted a victory for the radicals, since the new committee was composed of fewer conservatives and Tories than the old committee. Among the twenty-nine carry-overs into the Committee of Sixty were, besides Peter Van Schaack, John Jay, James Duane, Isaac Sears, and Alexander MacDougall. The Committee of Sixty proceeded to enforce the Continental Association vigorously. William Smith apparently remained behind the scenes as an adviser to the radicals, MacDougall and Sears.[63]

The Maryland Convention to which Robert Alexander had been elected in January, 1775 instituted a committee to which Alexander was appointed to "contract for exporting Provisions and other Produce . . . and . . . in Return to import Arms, Ammunition, Sulphur and Salt Petre according to the Recommendation of the Continental Congress."[64] Again Robert Alexander and Daniel Dulany came into conflict. Dulany opposed the raising and arming of troops by the Convention. This, he believed, was "not proper" because Maryland already possessed a "Constitutional Militia" whose officers were appointed by the governor. The Convention was attempting to supersede this militia with an extra-legal army that was not under the control or authority of the legitimate provincial government. As a member of the Council, Dulany had taken an oath to uphold the

[61] Kenneth Shipton, *Sibley's Harvard Graduates*, XIII, 385.

[62] *4: Amer. Arch.*, I, 330. Becker, *Political Parties*, 167.

[63] See for example: Diary entries, March 18 and March 20, 1775; *WS Diary* I, 214.

[64] Johnson, *Robert Alexander*, 61.

existing government, "therefore any assistance, directly, or indirectly, in the Execution of the proposed measure, would be I think a Violation of my Oath."[65] This letter, written to the Committee of Anne Arundel County, brought the wrath of the radicals down upon Dulany's head and he found it necessary to keep an armed guard at his house for several weeks. Dulany found himself in the middle of an explosive situation. He considered the Coercive Acts to be unconstitutional and therefore illegal violations of colonial rights. However, he refused to resist them because Parliament was the supreme legitimate governing body in the empire even though it had promulgated and was attempting to enforce unconstitutional measures. On the other hand, although he agreed in theory with the actions of the first Continental Congress, he refused to obey its dictates or the orders of the Maryland Convention because he considered them to be self-appointed, extra-legal bodies with no constitutional foundation for their actions.

Even before the adjournment of the first Continental Congress, New England began to prepare for war. On September 1, 1774, British troops from Boston marched to Cambridge and Charlestown and seized munitions belonging to the Commonwealth of Massachusetts that were stored there. With this action it became only a matter of time until war broke out. When on April 19, 1775, shots were fired at Lexington and Concord all of the colonies prepared for war. Dr. Benjamin Church had participated in the Battle of Lexington where he urged the militia on and must have been in the thick of the fighting for he was splattered with blood from a man who was killed next to him.[66] At the time he was chairman of the Committee of Safety and in May signed Benedict Arnold's commission for the attack on Fort Ticonderoga. As evidence of his martial

[65] Daniel Dulany to the Committee of Anne Arundel County, January 16, 1775; Dulany Papers, Maryland Historical Society.
[66] Paul Revere to the Corresponding Secretary, January 1, 1798; *Collections* of the Massachusetts Historical Society, series 1, V, 110–111.

spirit he was appointed by the Provincial Congress to confer with the Continental Congress. Church's mission was to secure congressional direction for the New England armies which were gathered before Boston. As a direct result of his appearances before Congress George Washington was appointed to command the army.[67] In July, 1775 Church himself entered the army as Director General and Chief Physician of the first Army Hospital at Cambridge, Massachusetts with a salary of $4 *per diem*. It is probable that his appointment stemmed from his appearance before Congress, although he was a fine physician.

Yet, at this high point in his career Dr. Benjamin Church was exposed, on September 30, 1775, as a Loyalist spy. A coded letter which he had written to his Loyalist brother-in-law John Fleming was intercepted when his mistress, charged with delivering the letter, gave it to the wrong man. Dr. Church was court martialled by General Washington and found guilty of "holding criminal correspondence with the enemy." He was imprisoned, but after the British evacuation of Boston was placed on parole because his health was bad.[68]

There is little direct evidence of Church's treason, but from the circumstantial evidence it appears as if Church were guilty. As early as January, 1772 Governor Hutchinson wrote that Church was writing political tracts for the government.[69] But there is no proof of this allegation. It seems likely that some of the "liberty songs" that Dr. Church wrote were misinterpreted by the governor. The songs were satirical and ironical and dotted with double meanings. It is probable that Hutchinson read the government's point of view into them. It is likely however that Church became a spy for General Gage sometime early in 1775, although there is no method by which the date can be pinpointed. After a careful study of all the known

---

[67] French, *General Gage's Informers*, 155.

[68] *Ibid.*, 190. *D. A. B.*, IV, 100–101.

[69] Thomas Hutchinson to Francis Bernard, January 29, 1772; Shipton, *Harvard Graduates*, XIII, 384.

letters by spies to General Gage, Allen French has concluded that none of them were in Church's handwriting.[70]

There are however, aside from the intercepted letter which was fairly innocuous, two pieces of evidence which point to Dr. Church's guilt. He was appointed to go to Philadelphia to secure congressional direction for the armies on May 16, 1775. He was to be the sole delegate and was not appointed as part of a committee. The next letter which Gage received from his spy arrived on May 24. The author of the letter stated: "I am appointed to my vexation to carry the dispatches to Philadelphia, & must set out tomorrow."[71] This is evidence that, although the letter is not in Church's hand, he was Gage's correspondent. The second piece of evidence is even more indirect. In January, 1778 Church was released by the Americans in an exchange of prisoners and after his death his wife and family received a sizable pension from the crown "in consequence of *certain services* he had rendered government."[72] Church died in January, 1778 in a shipwreck on his way to exile in England.

The arrest of Dr. Benjamin Church and revelation of his crimes caused an immediate shocked reaction in Massachusetts. If a man as trusted as the Surgeon General of the Continental Army was a spy, who could be trusted? Rumors began to circulate that John Adams was also a traitor and that John Hancock had embarked on a vessel of the Royal Navy before he too could be arrested.[73] The reaction of John Adams was typical:

I stand astonished. A Man of Genius, of Learning, of Family, of Character, a Writer of Liberty Songs and good ones too, a Speaker of Liberty orations, a Member of the Boston Committee of Correspondence, a Member of the Massachusetts Congress, an Agent for that Congress to the Continental Con-

---

[70] French, *General Gage's Informers*, 115.
[71] *Ibid.*, 156–157.
[72] *Ibid.*, 158.
[73] Catherine D. Bowen, *John Adams and the American Revolution* (pb. edn., New York, n.d.), 550.

gress, a Member of the House, a Director General of the
Hospital and Surgeon General—Good God! What shall We
say of human Nature? What shall We say of American
Patriots?[74]

Reaction to the events of April 19, 1775, in New York City
was immediate. News of the fighting reached New York on
April 23rd. By the next day, according to William Smith,

> The Populace had seized the City Arms after demanding the
> Key & the Magazene . . . and taken out 12 hundd Weight of
> Powder & threatened to attack 406 Soldiers under the Com-
> mand of Major Hamilton.[75]

Because of the changing circumstances of the conflict with
Great Britain, leadership of the struggle was placed in the
hands of a committee that was organized on May 1, 1775, with
100 members. Peter Van Schaack was a member, joining such
radicals as Alexander MacDougall and John Morin Scott.[76] The
association of this committee was written by three of its members, James Duane, John Jay and Peter Van Schaack, who
declared that the committee would

> adopt and endeavor to carry into execution whatever mea-
> sures may be recommended by the Continental Congress, or
> resolved upon by our Provincial Convention, for the purpose
> of preserving our Constitution and opposing the execution
> of the several arbitrary and oppressive Acts of the British
> Parliament.[77]

On May 2, 1775 Van Schaack was appointed to the Committee
of Correspondence and Intelligence along with the leading

---

[74] French, *General Gage's Informers*, 195–196. For a discussion of the
reasons for Church's treason see below, chapter six.
[75] Diary entry, April 24, 1775; *WS Diary* I, 221. The entry for April
25 puts the number of soldiers at 106. This is probably the correct figure.
[76] *New York Colonial Documents*, VIII, 600.
[77] Becker, *Political Parties*, 196–197.

Patriots of New York.[78] That Peter Van Schaack was considered to be a Patriot at this time is beyond doubt. He firmly believed that the dispute could not be settled until all powers of taxation were given up by Great Britain. "With respect to Massachusetts Bay: theirs is considered as a *common cause*, and therefore no peace can be established, till the acts relative to them are repealed." He believed that when the second Continental Congress met, its recommendations and actions would "have the force of more than *Law*."[79]

In Maryland Robert Alexander consolidated his political position in much the same fashion as Peter Van Schaack had. During the year 1775 Alexander served as the Secretary of the Baltimore Committee of Observation and on May 18 was elected a delegate to the Provincial Convention.[80] In June he became one of the three Commissioners of the Watch which had been established by the Committee of Observation to patrol the town of Baltimore.[81] On August 29 he subscribed to the "Association of the Freemen of Maryland" which declared that it was "necessary and justifiable" for the colonies to oppose Great Britain by force of arms.[82] This action was preceded by Alexander's election to the Maryland Council of Safety where he interested himself in the acquisition of armaments. Early in August he began to send agents to Bermuda and the West Indies to explore the possibilities of exchanging provisions for muskets and gunpowder.[83] By the end of the month the Council of Safety voted to give Robert Alexander full power to contract for the manufacture and purchase of

---

[78] *4: Amer. Arch.*, II, 471.

[79] Peter Van Cchaack to Col. John Maunsell, May 7, 1775; Van Schaack, *Peter Van Schaack*, 37–39.

[80] Scharf, *Chronicles of Baltimore*, 133. Johnson, *Robert Alexander*, 48.

[81] Johnson, *Robert Alexander*, 50–51.

[82] *4: Amer. Arch.*, III, 131, 448. *Archives of Maryland: Journal of the Maryland Convention July 26–August 14, 1775; Journal and Correspondence of the Maryland Council of Safety August 29, 1775–July 6, 1776* (ed. William Hand Browne; vol. XI, Baltimore, 1892), 74.

[83] Robert Alexander to ?, August 5, 1775; Gilmore Papers, Maryland Historical Society.

muskets, ammunition and other military equipment and paid him $7000 for that purpose.[84]

Even Daniel Dulany, a moderate who disapproved of the use of force, was caught up in the revolutionary fervor to some extent. In February, 1776 he consented to allow the Maryland Convention to erect iron mills for the production of munitions on property he controlled. This seems to have been a voluntary action on his part.[85]

Although he became prominent, due to his family connection, at an earlier date than either Robert Alexander or Peter Van Schaack, Andrew Allen occupied a very similar position to that of these two men in 1775. Allen had been Attorney General of Pennsylvania since November, 1769 and held the post until 1776 when the proprietary government was superseded. In 1770 and 1771 he had been a member of the Provincial Council. During the year 1774 Andrew Allen was appointed or elected to several other important posts. In May he was appointed, along with James Tilghman, a commissioner to regulate the Virginia–Pennsylvania boundary line and in June was elected Recorder of Philadelphia. Allen seems to have been in a martial frame of mind even before the start of war, for he was one of the founders and the first lieutenant of the First Troop of the Philadelphia City Cavalry. When war broke out in Massachusetts the Pennsylvania Assembly, on June 30, 1775, appointed Andrew Allen a member of the Council of Safety for the defense of the province.[86]

Allen's original appointments and elections to public office may possibly be attributed to the influence of the Allen family in Pennsylvania politics, but Andrew proved to be an extremely capable individual. In the Council of Safety he concerned himself primarily with military affairs, as did Robert Alexander in Maryland. When Pennsylvania decided to raise an army for

[84] 4: *Amer. Arch.,* III, 448–449.

[85] Land, *Dulanys of Maryland,* 321.

[86] Charles P. Keith, "Andrew Allen," *Pennsylvania Magazine of History and Biography* (X, 1886, 361–365), 362–363.

the defense of the province in August, 1775, Andrew Allen, Benjamin Franklin and five other members of the Council of Safety were appointed to draw up rules and regulations for the Associated Militia.[87]

Both Andrew Allen and Robert Alexander must have done well as members of the Councils of Safety, for before the end of 1775 both were elected delegates to the Continental Congress: Andrew Allen by the Pennsylvania Assembly on November 3, and Robert Alexander by the Maryland Provincial Convention on December 9.[88] Alexander took his seat in Congress early in January, 1776 after having received very specific instructions from the Convention. He and the other Maryland delegates were "to secure the Colonies against the exercise of the right assumed by Parliament to tax them, and to alter and change the Charters, Constitutions, and internal policy, without their consent—powers incompatible with the essential securities of the colonists." But while doing this, the Maryland delegates were not "without the previous knowledge and approbation of the Convention of this Province, [to] assent to any proposition to declare these Colonies independent of the Crown of *Great Britain*, nor to any proposition for making or entering into alliance with any foreign Power, nor to any union or confederation of these colonies which may necessarily lead to a separation from the mother country." They were, however, given permission to join with the other colonies "in such military operations as may be judged proper and necessary for the common defense."[89] Robert Alexander was in firm agreement with these instructions. He wrote that "they intirely coincide with my Judgment & that Line of Conduct which I had de-

---

[87] *Minutes of the Provisional Council of Pennsylvania, from the Organization to the Termination of Proprietary Government. . . . Vol. X. . . . Minutes of the Council of Safety from June 30, 1775, to November 12, 1776* (Harrisburg, Pennsylvania, 1852), 297. Hereafter cited as: *Minutes of the [Pa.] Council of Safety.*

[88] *4: Amer. Arch.,* III, 1908, 1956.

[89] *Ibid.,* IV, 463–464.

termined to persue." According to John Dickinson, to whom Alexander showed his instructions, "they breath that Spirit, which ought to govern all publick Bodies, Firmness tempered with Moderation."[90]

Both Robert Alexander and Andrew Allen seem to have served as liaisons between their respective Committees of Safety and the Congress, primarily with regard to the purchase and manufacture of munitions. Alexander was appointed a member of the Secret Committee on January 16, 1776, and a member of the Marine Committee on April 12.[91] Appointment to the Secret Committee was a great honor for a new Congressman. It was an executive department of Congress with nine members who were empowered to contract for the importation of powder and munitions. The name of the committee stemmed from the fact that its members were given the authority to conceal committee operations from the Congress as a whole. The Marine Committee functioned as a naval department and was in charge of the Continental Navy. Robert Alexander was in close touch with the supply problems confronting America in its attempts to build a military establishment. He constantly urged Maryland to erect a gunpowed factory since he could supply the Council of Safety, through the Continental Congress, with the saltpetre necessary for its manufacture. He firmly believed that it was necessary for the colonies to manufacture their own munitions, for "if we rely on foreign arms & they are not better than the sample we have, our dependance will be like a broken reed, as I think if used, they will kill more of our Troops than the Enemy."[92]

Andrew Allen was a member of various committees in Con-

---

[90] Robert Alexander to the Maryland Council of Safety, January 30, 1776; *Archives of Maryland*, XI, 133.

[91] *Journals of the Continental Congress, 1774–1789* (ed. Worthington C. Ford; 34 vols., Washington, 1904–1937), IV, 59, 275.

[92] Robert Alexander to the Maryland Council of Safety, February 16, 1776; *Archives of Maryland*, XI, 164.

gress, notably the Committee of Five for the procurement of cannon, the committee to superintend the printing of the journals of Congress, and the Committee of Three to supervise the defense of New York City. This committee had the authority to issue orders to General Lee in preparing the city for defense.[93] While Robert Alexander was urging Maryland to manufacture gunpowder, Andrew Allen faced a somewhat similar situation with regard to Pennsylvania. Pennsylvania produced most of the gunpowder that was manufactured in the colonies. Soon after his appointment to Congress Andrew Allen, upon instructions from the Marine Committee, began to ask the Pennsylvania Committee of Safety to donate gunpowder for the use of the Continental Army.[94] The shortage of gunpowder in the colonies was acute and both Alexander and Allen did all they could to alleviate the shortage.

Andrew Allen seems to have received the approbation of the people of Philadelphia. On May 20, 1776, he was elected to the Pennsylvania Assembly by Philadelphia and now held four important posts in the province: Assemblyman, Congressman, member of the Committee of Safety and Attorney General of Pennsylvania.[95] Robert Alexander became a more thoroughgoing radical because of his services in Congress. When he was appointed to Congress his instructions included a prohibition on independence. Alexander thoroughly approved of this. In February, 1776 a committee of the Congress composed of Alexander, John Dickinson, James Wilson and James Duane wrote an address to the inhabitants of the United Colonies in which they disavowed all thoughts of independence by Congress.[96] Yet, within two weeks Robert Alexander began

---

[93] *Journals of the Continental Congress,* IV, 55, 94, 224.

[94] *4: Amer. Arch.,* III, 1835–1836.

[95] *Ibid.,* IV, 845.

[96] John Henry Edmunds, "How Massachusetts Received the Declaration of Independence," *Proceedings* of the American Antiquarian Society (XXXV, 1925, 227–252), 229–230.

to advocate independence. His about face was explained by receipt of the news of Lord North's Conciliatory Act. As he wrote:

> What Measures Congress may pursue in Consequence of this Act, I know not. With me every Idea of Reconciliation is precluded by the conduct of G. Britain, & the only alternitave, absolute Slavery or Independency. The latter I have often reprobated both in public & private, but am now almost convinced the Measure is right & can be justified by necessity.[97]

Although Allen and Alexander increased in importance and position in 1775 and 1776, many of the men who were to become Whig-Loyalists began to suffer a decline in the importance of their political and social leadership. William Samuel Johnson is a case in point. In December, 1774 he was appointed a member of the Committee of Inspection in Stratford, Connecticut and still retained a seat in the Connecticut Council. His popularity began to decline soon after the Battle of Lexington when he and Erastus Wolcott were sent to General Gage by the Connecticut Assembly to plead for a suspension of hostilities. The mission was misunderstood by the Massachusetts authorities and although he and Wolcott were allowed into Boston and returned to Connecticut, Johnson was never fully trusted by the radicals after the episode.[98] He stopped attending meetings of the Council, but did not officially resign his seat until July 4, 1776, when he retired to Stratford. His conduct must have been in harmony with local sentiment in Stratford for he was reelected to the Committee of Inspection in December, 1775.[99] Although the Assembly appointed him, on December 14, 1775, to a committee charged with procuring an account of the damages done by English troops in Connecticut, it is

---

[97] Robert Alexander to the Maryland Council of Safety, February 27, 1776; *Archives of Maryland*, XI, 188–190.

[98] Beardsley, *William Samuel Johnson*, 109.

[99] Groce, *William Samuel Johnson*, 102.

obvious that Johnson no longer commanded the attention of the Patriots as he had in the early 1770's. After this last appointment he virtually disappeared from the public scene.

Peter Van Schaack's decline from political leadership began soon after his election to the Committee of One-Hundred. It was probably caused more by reasons of health than by any change in his political views at the time. Some time during the month of May, 1775, he and his family moved from New York City to their old home at Kinderhook where Peter Van Schaack had been born. According to Van Schaack's biographer, the reason for the move was the fact that his wife and children were in poor health, while Peter himself was slowly going blind.[100] Apparently the failure of his eyesight, probably due to cataracts, caused a falling off of his law practice. He could neither read nor study for long periods of time. In September he justified the move to Kinderhook to his father-in-law, using the loss of his practice as the excuse.[101] Peter Van Schaack's reputation preceded him to Kinderhook, for soon after his arrival he was elected a member of the Committee of Safety, Correspondence and Protection of Albany County.[102] But he never became an active member of the committee as his eyesight grew progressively weaker. By the spring of 1776 he had become completely blind in the right eye and had extremely poor vision in the left.[103] But it is obvious that although Van Schaack had forsaken active participation in the Whig cause, he had not lost his patriotic fervor. In December, 1775 when Isaac Sears led the New York mob against James Rivington's printing office, Van Schaack crowed at their success and called Rivington, who published a Tory newspaper, the "Enemy."[104]

---

[100] Van Schaack, *Peter Van Schaack*, 51.

[101] Peter Van Schaack to Henry Cruger, Sr., September 6, 1775; Peter Van Schaack Papers, Columbia University Library.

[102] Van Schaack, *Peter Van Schaack*, 58.

[103] *Ibid.*

[104] Peter Van Schaack to William Laight, December 19, 1775; Peter Van Schaack Papers, Columbia University Library.

One of the reasons for the loss of political leadership and influence on the part of some of the leading Patriots was their response to the shooting war. All of the Whig-Loyalists, with the exception of Daniel Leonard, were willing to oppose Great Britain verbally and through the use of economic sanctions, but some of them were not willing to take up arms against the mother country. As early as 1769 William Samuel Johnson perfectly expressed these sentiments when he wrote: "I would not serve the people against the Crown nor can I the Crown against the people."[105] After April 19, 1775, this pacifist viewpoint placed William Samuel Johnson at something of a disadvantage when it came to political action. While he was persuaded to travel to Boston to ask General Gage to end hostilities, he could not be persuaded to retain his seat in the Connecticut Council and aid in the prosecution of the American resistance to Great Britain.

William Smith, while also becoming a moderate by 1775, was willing to raise a call to arms, believing that America would do so "merely for her Defense—and in Resisting oppression, she will not oppress. . . . We are Soldiers to obtain the Rights of Citizens."[106] He did not believe that the struggle was one of independence or slavery, but thought that America would lay down her arms once she had achieved her goals in taxation and legislation. Believing thus, William Smith was able to write to a correspondent in England in October, 1775:

> The dread of our being taxed by the Commons of Great Britain, is the Soul of the League, that bands the Provinces together. Give them a constitutional Security ag[ains]t Arbitrary Levies; that is to say, covenant that they shall be Englishmen, and the Advocates for Independency, will be found such a Handful, even in the most suspected Colonies,

---

[105] William Samuel Johnson to N. Rogers, April 22, 1769; Bancroft Transcripts, William Samuel Johnson Correspondence.

[106] Diary entry, July 3, 1775; WS *Diary* I, 232–233.

that they may be left to the Correction of the Rest of their own Countrymen.[107]

It is natural that Robert Alexander and Andrew Allen were much more radical than either Smith or Johnson when it came to the shooting war. Both men had risen to power during the pre-revolutionary struggles. Although the basis for Allen's power was vested in legal offices, he also profited from his family's opposition to the Quaker Party and because the Presbyterian Party was identified with the national Whig cause. Similarly, Alexander's rise was based on opposition to England. Because of the difference between the two proprietary governments of Pennsylvania and Maryland, Alexander's rise to prominence was also predicated on opposition to the proprietary. In Congress, Robert Alexander busied himself with work concerning the war. In January, 1776 he was involved with drawing up plans for the reduction of Sir Guy Carleton and his troops.[108] He also served on the committee which supervised most of the arms purchases for the Continental Army. He often had occasion to complain that, for many, "Patriotism sinks before private interest, and I find many men here, who rank themselves in that class, generally exacting the most from the necessity of their country, hence the publick is plundered."[109]

Andrew Allen was involved with the Pennsylania militia as early as June, 1775 but had been a member of the Philadelphia militia before that time. On June 30, 1775, a twenty-five-man Committee of Safety was appointed by the Assembly with such men as Benjamin Franklin, John Dickinson, Anthony Wayne, Robert Morris and Andrew Allen as members. Its duties were to "provide for the Defense of this Province against insurrec-

---

[107] William Smith to General Haldimand, October 6, 1775; *ibid.*, 240.
[108] Robert Alexander to the Maryland Council of Safety, January 30, 1776; *4: Amer. Arch.*, IV, 887.
[109] Robert Alexander to the Maryland Council of Safety, February 16, 1776; *Archives of Maryland*, XI, 164.

tion and Invasion."[110] When Andrew Allen became a member of the Continental Congress he served as a link between the two bodies and helped to keep them in harmony with one another.

In the period before the Declaration of Independence the first real break with the Patriots was made by some of the Whigs under discussion. Daniel Dulany maintained his position as a moderate and did not change his political views to any great degree. He remained the epitome of what may be called the Whig-Loyalist. Dulany, at the time of the first Continental Congress, was joined in this position by William Samuel Johnson, Dr. Benjamin Church and Daniel Leonard. Johnson became a moderate Whig-Loyalist, Leonard took a more conservative stand, and Church became an active Loyalist. During the period Leonard's views became similar, but not identical, to those of Thomas Hutchinson and Jared Ingersoll, while Johnson's and Dulany's opinions about the Coercive Acts and the congresses were much more moderate and Whiggish in tone. Four of the Whigs under discussion became Whig-Loyalists before the Declaration of Independence, and others maintained their positions as radical or moderate Patriots, although Peter Van Schaack declined in political activity. William Smith was a moderate who retained the trust of the radicals, not only in New York, but of John Adams as well.[111] Andrew Allen and Robert Alexander were leading radicals. Through this period there is no way of distinguishing their views on the crisis with England from those of such men as John Adams, Alexander MacDougall, or other leaders of the Sons of Liberty. Nor can William Smith's or Peter Van Schaack's views be distinguished from the views of moderate Whigs such as John Dickinson of Pennsylvania.

110 *Minutes of the* [Pa.] *Council of Safety*, 280.
111 Diary entry, August 22, 1774; Adams, *Works*, II, 349.

6

THE CRISIS OF INDEPENDENCE

Even before the Declaration of Independence several of the men we are discussing began to consider themselves to be Loyalists, although only two, Dr. Benjamin Church and Daniel Leonard, became open supporters of British imperial policy. It would be erroneous to state that they began to switch their allegiance from America to Great Britain. During the Stamp Act crisis such men as William Smith and Daniel Dulany, along with most Americans, considered themselves to be Englishmen in America, with English rights and liberties in a special American setting. As the gulf between England and her colonies widened, the Whig-Loyalists tried to cling to this view. But the actions in Congress of July 2–4, 1776, caused all of these men to face the supreme crisis of their lives. For the Tories the Declaration of Independence was not a crisis. Thomas Hutchinson had been predicting such a move since the time of the Stamp Act. The actual declaration just brought the basic motivation of the Patriots into the open. But for the Whig-Loyalists, and for many Americans, the Declaration of Independence meant that they would have to choose between either England or America. No longer could they consider themselves to be Englishmen, born in America, fighting for the rights of Englishmen. They had to decide whether they were

155

English or American. How the Whig-Loyalists met this challenge, and why, is the subject of this chapter.

The Declaration of Independence presented no problem whatever for Daniel Leonard or Dr. Benjamin Church. By July 4, 1776, Leonard was in Halifax, Nova Scotia with General Howe, having left Boston with the British troops in March. Soon after his departure, with the approval of his father, Colonel Ephraim Leonard, a staunch Patriot, Daniel Leonard was proscribed by Massachusetts, forbidden to return under penalty of death, and his property was confiscated.[1] When the British left Halifax for New York City, Leonard sailed for England. During the same period Dr. Benjamin Church was in prison as a consequence of his actions in 1775. However just before July 4, 1776, he was placed on parole in Massachusetts, an outcast in his own land. Due to threats it was feared that he would be killed if left at large and so he was again jailed, this time for his own protection.

It is interesting that three of the four Whig-Loyalists who had been to England compromised their ideals to some extent and remained in America, although they disapproved of independence. These three were William Byrd III, William Samuel Johnson and Daniel Dulany. William Byrd III was one of the finest military commanders the colonies produced during the French and Indian War. His military reputation was acknowledged throughout the colonies and, early in 1775, Byrd was offered the position of commander of the Virginia militia.[2] This offer placed Byrd in a predicament. Although he had opposed the British measures and British policy relating to the colonies, Byrd had spent several years in England. Two of his sons, Thomas Taylor Byrd and Francis Otway Byrd,

[1] William Reed Deane, *A Genealogical Memoir of The Leonard Family* (Boston, 1851), 10–11.

[2] William Byrd III to Sir Jeffrey Amherst, July 30, 1775; *Virginia Magazine of History and Biography*, XIX, 313. This letter constitutes the only known evidence of the fact that Byrd had been offered the command of the Virginia forces, although there is a tradition to that effect.

were members of the British armed services. Thomas Taylor Byrd was an officer in the British army at the seige of Boston. Four days before the British army evacuated the city, he wrote requesting his father to purchase a commission for him as a company commander.[3] The other son, Francis Otway Byrd, served in the Royal Navy aboard the *Fowey*, Sir George Montagu commanding, which was stationed at Hampton Roads, Virginia.[4] Apparently Francis did not enjoy service in the Royal Navy and was a patriotic Virginian, for by February, 1775 he was begging his father to use his considerable influence to get him out of the Royal Navy.[5] William Byrd III must have succeeded, for by May, 1776 Francis had been commissioned a captain in the Continental Army.[6] And so, William Byrd faced the task of either giving up his allegiance to the king and alienating one of his sons, or serving the king and alienating the other.

This quandary vexed Byrd for a time. He was an established member of the Virginia aristocracy and had been a member of the Council since 1768. In 1775 Virginia was presenting a united front towards England, as most of the Virginia aristocracy supported the measures being taken by Congress. If William Byrd accepted command of the Virginia militia he would have maintained this front. But he refused "to oppose the King's troops," although he believed that war was inevitable between England and the colonies. With this action William Byrd III became a Loyalist. He remained at his home of Westover where he "met with insults and [had] given offense because of his refusal to command the army being raised by the Convention." Nonetheless, Byrd asked Sir Jeffrey Amherst not to consider him to be "one of the American traitors as he [was] ready to serve his Majesty and would be

---

[3] Thomas Taylor Byrd to William Byrd III, June 11, 1775; Francis Otway Byrd Papers, Virginia Historical Society.

[4] Francis Otway Byrd to William Byrd III, October 11, 1774; *ibid*.

[5] Francis Otway Byrd to William Byrd III, February 10, 1775; *ibid*.

[6] Francis Otway Byrd to William Byrd III, May 6, 1776; *ibid*.

glad of an opportunity to convince Virginians of their error
& bring them back to loyalty and duty."[7] In fact he did nothing to aid the British cause and remained at Westover in
retirement. It is probable that he would not have taken up
arms for the crown despite his letter to Amherst. Many of his
friends and his son were serving in the colonial cause and as
late as April, 1776 Byrd retained the trust of radical Virginians
of his own social standing. On April 17th Charles Lee wrote
to William Byrd to express the "very great esteem and warm
affection" he had for William Byrd. He went on to discuss
military affairs with Byrd and explored the possibilities of a
declaration of independence. In the letter he seems to have
assumed that Byrd was undecided on the question of independence and sought to persuade him. Lee wrote:

> Our political disputes now intirely turn on [   ] / or inde-
> pendence. As the latter appears to [   ] / -vitable, the
> sooner, in my opinion, it comes the better, as a speedy
> declaration must [   ] / infinite effusion of blood and
> money.[8]

After the Declaration of Independence, however, Byrd became
despondent and began to drink a great deal more than he had
heretofore, although his personal and business affairs improved
during the 1770's. On New Year's day, 1777, at the age of
forty-eight, William Byrd III committed suicide at Westover.[9]
    The experiences of Daniel Dulany and William Samuel
Johnson were not so dramatic but do show the trials and tribu-
lations that the Whig-Loyalists were forced to undergo in the
period immediately following the Declaration of Independence.
Daniel Dulany experienced a family conflict which was similar
to the one that William Byrd III had undergone: the type

---

[7] William Byrd III to Sir Jeffrey Amherst, July 30, 1775; *op cit.*
[8] Charles Lee to William Byrd III, April 17, 1776; Brock Collection, Huntington Library. (The letter is mutilated so that about one word is missing at the end of each line.)
[9] *Virginia Magazine of History and Biography,* XIII, 229.

of family conflict that turned the American Revolution into a civil war for many families. Two of Dulany's sons and one of his nephews became Tories and actively opposed the authority of the Maryland Convention before leaving the province for England during the summer of 1775.[10] Another son, Ben, was a Patriot.[11] Throughout the period Daniel Dulany played out the role that he thought he had created for himself after the repeal of the Stamp Act—that of a neutral, an independent thinker, and a legalist. He allowed the Maryland Convention to use his iron works for the manufacture of munitions, but Dulany always believed that the proprietary was the only legal and official government of Maryland and opposed the raising of troops by the Convention. In a letter to the Committee of Anne Arundel County Dulany stated:

> I do not assume any pretention to Controul the opinion of others, but I claim the right of judging freely, and of acting freely according to my Judgment. The raising of Troops is a measure I apprehend not proper; We have a Constitutional Militia composed of the Freemen of the Province. . . . The measure seems to me to be improper, because it effectually supersedes the Constitutional Militia.

He went on to write that his oath as a member of the Maryland Council and his own judgment forbade him to render any assistance to the committee.[12]

Dulany thereby found himself in the position of refusing actively to oppose Parliament or to obey the Continental Congress. When the Declaration of Independence was promulgated, Dulany refused to recognize the new order and retained his allegiance to the proprietary government of Maryland. But he came to terms with the actual government of the Maryland

---

[10] They were Daniel Dulany III, Lloyd Dulany and Daniel Dulany, son of Walter Dulany. Land, *Dulanys of Maryland,* 317.

[11] *Ibid.,* 323.

[12] Daniel Dulany to the Committee of Anne Arundel County, January 16, 1775; Dulany Papers, Maryland Historical Society.

Convention by remaining neutral and perpetrating no overt acts. He became, in effect, a passive Loyalist.

Because of the many years he had spent in England as Connecticut Agent, William Samuel Johnson had learned to appreciate the value of the common heritage that England and her American colonies shared. He believed that the mother country and her colonies were bound together not only by tradition but also by mutual economic interests. The severance of the ties between these areas would be a "shocking Catastrophe" and would spread "universal distress" in Great Britain and "desolution & calamity" in America.[13] Johnson was also pessimistic about America as an independent state. Writing from England in 1769 he had stated:

> If we were wise and could form some System of free Government upon just Principles we might be very happy without any Connection with this Country. But should we ever agree upon any thing of this Nature, should we not more probably fall into Factions and Parties amongst ourselves, destroy one another and become at length the easy prey Probably of the first Invaders.[14]

And so Johnson seems to have formed a preference for "Home Rule" with the "supreme power" of the empire in the hands of Parliament.[15]

After returning to Stratford from his mission to General Gage in 1775 Johnson, like Dulany, became a neutral. He went into retirement, "convinced that I could not join in a war against England and much less could I join in a war against my own country."[16] His retirement from public life became complete in June, 1776 when he failed to be reelected

---

[13] Quoted in Groce, *William Samuel Johnson*, 90.

[14] William Samuel Johnson to Benjamin Gale, April 10, 1769; William Samuel Johnson Papers, Connecticut Historical Society.

[15] William Samuel Johnson to Nathaniel Rogers, November 15, 1769; *ibid.*

[16] Quoted in Oscar Zeichner, *Connecticut's Years of Controversy 1750–1776* (Chapel Hill, 1949), 352.

to the Council. The Declaration of Independence meant little to him in his role as a neutral. He continued with his law practice until November, 1777, when the state of Connecticut required all officers of the court to take an oath of allegiance to Connecticut as a free and independent state. Johnson refused to take the oath and was compelled to give up his practice.[17] He was now considered to be not simply a neutral, but a Loyalist.

Robert Alexander and Andrew Allen, as members of Congress, had a closer connection with the Declaration of Independence than any of the other Whig-Loyalists. Pennsylvania developed an interesting situation early in 1776 which changed Andrew Allen from a radical into a moderate. In Pennsylvania the regularly constituted Assembly of the proprietary government maintained its control over provincial affairs, much to the consternation of some of the radicals. The Pennsylvania Council of Safety had been appointed by the Assembly and as such was more amenable to moderating influences than were the Sons of Liberty. Because he was Governor Penn's brother-in-law, Andrew Allen became one of the targets of the radicals. They believed that he would not vote for independence since he was a member of the Council and closely connected with the Penn family.[18] When on May 15, 1776, the Continental Congress resolved that the colonies which had not already organized governments of their own choosing should do so, the Pennsylvania Assembly, to which Andrew Allen had just been elected, appointed him chairman of a committee to draw up a remonstrance.[19] The move by Congress had been a calculated effort to get the more reluctant colonies, such as Pennsylvania, to proceed towards independence; but it had the effect of alienating men like Allen.

---

[17] Groce, *William Samuel Johnson,* 106.
[18] See; Edward Shippen to Jasper Yeates, March 11, 1776; Yeates Papers, Historical Society of Pennsylvania.
[19] *Pennsylvania Magazine of History and Biography,* LXXVIII, 1954, 14–15.

Andrew Allen, because of his actions in Congress, was considered to be extremely virulent against the power of Great Britain, but when it came to the question of independence he backed off.[20] Just one month after the Congressional resolve mentioned above, Andrew Allen stopped attending sessions of Congress, believing that there was nothing he could do to avert a declaration of independence. He was willing, as we have seen, to fight England in order to defend American rights, but he was not willing for America to leave the British empire. In keeping with this view Allen was not content to sit back and be a neutral as were Daniel Dulany and William Samuel Johnson; neither was he content to sit out the war in England as Daniel Leonard had chosen to do. Allen felt that he had to fight for his beliefs and with his brothers, who believed as he did and followed his lead, went to New York City in January, 1777, renounced the oaths he had taken as a member of the Continental Congress, and took an oath of allegiance to the king.[21] His brothers did the same. John Allen had been a member of the New Jersey Convention and William Allen, Jr. had been a lieutenant colonel in the Continental Army and had served in the Canadian campaign. All three brothers gave up their positions with the passage of the Declaration of Independence. The avowed loyalism of the Allen brothers caused a stir of excitement not only in Philadelphia, but in New York as well. William Smith considered their actions and political opinions to be very similar to his own since "they gave up their Places upon the Declaration of Independency."[22]

---

[20] American Loyalists, Transcript of the Manuscript Books and Papers of Commission of Enquiry into the Losses and Services of the American Loyalists held under Acts of Parliament of 23, 25, 28, and 29 of George III preserved amongst the Audit Office Records in the Public Record Office in England, 1783–1790. Sixty volumes on microfilm, New York Public Library, III, 401–403.

[21] Keith, "Andrew Allen," 363–364.

[22] Diary entry, January 7, 1777; William Smith, *Historical Memoirs from 12 July 1776 to 25 July 1778* (ed. William H. W. Sabine; New York, 1958), 62. Hereafter cited as *WS Diary* II.

Robert Alexander began to advocate independence as early as February, 1776 but he, like the Allen brothers, could not agree to a severance of the ties which bound the empire together when the Declaration of Independence was promulgated five months later. Yet, he retained the faith of the Maryland Convention for several months thereafter. On May 10, 1776 Congress

Resolved, That it be recommended to the respective assemblies and conventions of the United States, where no government sufficient to the exigencies of their affairs have been hitherto established, to adopt such government as shall, in the opinion of the representatives of the people, best conduce to the happiness and safety of their constituents in particular, and America in general.[23]

This action had caused the Pennsylvania Assembly to appoint a committee chaired by Andrew Allen to write a protest. Robert Alexander took more immediate action. He withdrew from Congress and declared that this resolve was "equivalent to a dicln of independence."[24]

Alexander's action was not ill thought of in Maryland, for on May 21, and again on July 4, he was reelected to the Continental Congress.[25] But he did not accept either of these appointments. Apparently his health was not good, for on his return to Baltimore in June the Maryland Council of Safety congratulated him on his return and hoped that he would soon be "restored to perfect health."[26] Alexander apparently used an injury to his leg as an excuse to avoid attending, not only Congress, but also meetings of the Maryland Convention. In a letter to the President of the Convention he asked to be

[23] *Journals of the Continental Congress,* IV, 341–342.
[24] American Loyalists, Commission of Enquiry, XXXVI, 170.
[25] *Proceedings of the Conventions of . . . Maryland . . . in 1774, 1775 & 1776* (Baltimore, 1836), 141, 189.
[26] Maryland Council of Safety to Robert Alexander, June 12, 1776; *Archives of Maryland,* XI, 487.

excused from attendance because "the wound in my ankle has hitherto and still continues to disable me. Since last Sunday week I have not been out of my house, and it is with difficulty and great pain I can even walk from one room to another." He hoped that his absence would be excusable because "duty to my constituents and inclination both prompt me to join in the councils of my country, and more especially at this very interesting period."[27] This letter, in view of Alexander's later actions, seems to have been written with tongue in cheek.

On August 19, Alexander was brought before the Baltimore County Committee where it was charged that he had "uttered several reprehensible expressions in a speech made to the people at the close of the polls for delegates from Baltimore County in the Provincial Congress."[28] He did not deny the charges and later declared that he had expressed "his Sentiments on the Politicks of the times avowing his Opposition to Independence."[29] In September, 1776 he refused to take an oath renouncing all allegiance to Great Britain and was barred from the practice of law. He therefore left Baltimore with his family and retired to his estate in Cecil County.[30]

Robert Alexander had no intention of leaving his considerable property in Maryland. In 1777 George Washington caused a furor in Maryland by dining at Robert Alexander's home, although the general did not know that Alexander was now considered to be a "Tory." During the course of conversation Washington discovered this fact and asked: "Do you mean to stay here, or are you going to move?" "I have made up my mind to stay," Alexander replied, "and I shall take all consequences."[31] But when General Howe landed in Maryland in September, 1777 Alexander entertained him. When Howe

---

[27] Robert Alexander to the President of the Maryland Convention, June 25, 1776; 4: *Amer. Arch.*, VI, 1063.

[28] 5: *Amer. Arch.*, I, 1056–1057.

[29] American Loyalists, Commission of Enquiry, XXXVI, 172–173.

[30] Johnson, *Robert Alexander*, 101.

[31] American Loyalists, Commission of Enquiry, XXXVI, 173.

was ready to leave, Alexander, fearing that he might be hanged by his irate neighbors, fled to New York City with Howe and "abandoned his family and fortune, leaving a Wife and six young children at the mercy of his Enemies."[32]

Both Peter Van Schaack and William Smith had reservations about independence and the course America was pursuing early in 1776. On May 15, 1776 both of these men were included in a list of persons suspected of having an "equivocal character" which was promulgated by the New York Provincial Congress.[33] Although he was a member of the Albany County Committee of Correspondence, Van Schaack began to have doubts about the American cause as early as January, 1776. The failure of Montgomery and Arnold's attack on Quebec filled him with joy.[34] Yet even though he was suspected by the Provincial Congress, Van Schaack was reelected to the Albany Committee, as a member for Kinderhook, on May 29.[35] On that day he attended his first meeting of the committee and refused to sign its general association which included a pledge to take up arms against England.[36] Peter Van Schaack objected to this part of the association. At the time he described himself as being a member of that class of men which was "disposed to go along with the Congress to a certain limited extent, hoping in that way to fix what they conceived to be the *rights* of their country upon the firmest foundation; but as soon as they found, that the views and designs of the American leaders rested in nothing short of a dissolution of the union between Great Britain and her Colonies, they refused any longer to participate in the public measures."[37] This statement could have been written, not only by Peter Van Schaack,

---

[32] *Ibid.*, 156–157.

[33] *4: Amer. Arch.*, VI, 1368.

[34] Peter Van Schaack to Henry Cruger, Sr., January 14, 1776; Peter Van Schaack Papers, Columbia University Library.

[35] *Minutes of the Albany Committee of Correspondence 1775–1778* (ed. James Sullivan; 2 vols., Albany, 1923–1925), I, 421.

[36] *Ibid.*, 423.

[37] Van Schaack, *Peter Van Schaack*, 60.

but by any one of the Whig-Loyalists. It is the clearest expression of the Whig-Loyalist position written during the period.

On June 14, 1776, Peter Van Schaack was ordered to return to New York City by the Provincial Congress, but through the intercession of the Albany Committee he was allowed to remain at Kinderhook.[38] In September, when he applied for a pass to travel around Albany County, it was refused. Van Schaack, practically blind, was considered to be a danger to the public safety.[39] He was again called before the committee on January 9, 1777, to take an oath of allegiance as a subject of the independent State of New York. He refused to take the required oath but was allowed to sign a parole stating that he would leave Kinderhook for exile in Boston within ten days.[40] Van Schaack wandered through New England for several months with several other exiles but finally, in April, 1777, was allowed to return to Kinderhook through the intercession of two of his oldest friends, John Jay and Governor George Clinton. He signed a parole on April 4, promising to "neither directly or indirectly do or say any thing to the prejudice of the American cause."[41] Peter Van Schaack was determined, for the sake of his wife who was critically ill, to maintain a neutral position. In August, 1777 he wrote:

> In civil wars, I hold it there can be *no neutrality;* in *mind* I mean. Every man must *wish* one side or the other to prevail. . . . The *ruling powers,* therefore, have a right to consider every person, who does not join them in action, as averse to them in opinions; which will appear the more reasonable, as civil commotions are of such a nature as to give life and activity to the most powerful affections of the human mind.

Have they then a right to *punish* a mere difference of

---

38 *Albany Committee Minutes,* I, 451–452.
39 *Ibid.,* 563.
40 *Ibid.,* 655.
41 Van Schaack, *Peter Van Schaack,* 479.

sentiment? By no means. Punishment, as such, is due only to overt acts, to the transgression of some known law; and that there may be a strict neutrality *in practice*, is beyond dispute.[42]

Mrs. Van Schaack's illness caused her husband much anguish and when, in March, 1778, she wished to return to her home in New York City to be near her family, he wrote to his friend John Jay. Van Schaack asked Jay to intercede with the governor for permission to pass into Loyalist New York.[43] Jay tried to satisfy Van Schaack's request, but it was rejected by Clinton. He wrote however: "Any services in my power, command; I mean never to forget my friends, however different our noses, or sentiments may be."[44] Jay was to keep this pledge to Van Schaack in later years. Soon after this exchange of letters Mrs. Van Schaack died and Peter no longer felt the necessity of neutrality. On June 13, 1778, a Banishing Act was passed by the Provincial Congress and Peter Van Schaack again was ordered to appear before its Committee of Conspiracies. Although the committee banished Van Schaack, all of the commissioners were friends of his, and one, Leonard Gansevoort, Jr., had studied law under Van Schaack. Gansevoort was Secretary of the Board of Commissioners and even while banishing his former teacher, maintained his friendship and offered to pay the debts that he owed Van Schaack. He was under no legal obligation to do so but felt that Van Schaack might have need of the money in England.[45] Governor Clinton tried to save Peter Van Schaack from banishment by arresting the proceedings against him. He claimed to have given Van Schaack permission to go to England for treatment of his blindness before passage of the Banishing Act. When this move failed, Clinton offered to

---

[42] *Ibid.*, 88.
[43] Peter Van Schaack to John Jay, March 18, 1778; *ibid.*, 95–96.
[44] John Jay to Peter Van Schaack, March 26, 1778; *ibid.*, 97.
[45] Leonard Gansevoort, Jr. to Peter Van Schaack, July 21, 1778; *ibid.*, 110.

consider Van Schaack as a paroled British prisoner to enable him to remain in Kinderhook on parole rather than be banished from New York State. Van Schaack refused the offer and went into exile.[46] From England Peter Van Schaack sympathized with America, believed that it would maintain its independence, but thought that independence would corrupt. In November, 1779 he wrote in England:

> America will perhaps never see such happy days as the past. They may be a great empire, and enjoy opulence; but that mediocrity between extreme poverty and luxurious riches made their condition substantially happy. There being but few offices, there was no scope for bribery, corruption, and the numerous train of evils which attend the venality of this country. Henceforth, having an empire of their own, the numerous train of offices will produce like effects as the same causes do here.[47]

During this period William Smith's actions closely resembled those of Peter Van Schaack. In December, 1775 Smith was offered a seat on the New York bench. He declined, informing "the Governor that I could not think of any office held under the Crown upon Terms odious to the People."[48] This was a difficult decision for Smith to make, for his highest ambition in life was to be a judge. In March, 1776 he moved his family to his home in Haverstraw, New York, because of the British evacuation of Boston. Contrary to public opinion he believed that the British Army had sailed for Halifax—as it actually had—but he was not willing to take the chance that rumors of the army's coming to New York City were true.[49] Yet on June 27, 1776 William Smith was summoned to appear before the Provincial Congress "as a person of equivocal char-

---

[46] *Ibid.*, 120.
[47] *Ibid.*, 244.
[48] Diary entry, December 19, 1775; WS *Diary* I, 254.
[49] Diary entry, March 23, 1776; *ibid.*, 270.

acter," because of his membership in the New York Council.[50]
Smith answered with a letter on July 4. In it he wrote:

> Before I retired in March to my Country House for the
> Summer Season I understood it to be the Opinion of the
> [Provincial] Congress that the Council ought not to be
> desired to take an active Part in these unhappy Disputes
> and were therefore exempted from military Services; and
> I do hereby give you my parol that you shall have no cause
> by any Act of Mine to suspect my Friendship to the Rights
> and Liberties of this Country, being determined to continue
> with the dearest Pledges I can give of my Attachment to
> her Fortunes & Interests with the Power of the Congress.[51]

This answer was fully acceptable to the committee.

Smith believed that the Declaration of Independence had
hurt the American cause. Congress had, to his way of think-
ing, sublimated "their Principles [and] are lessening their
Numbers" of supporters. He believed that it was not only
himself and the Allen brothers who had broken with Congress
over the question of independence, but that many others had
done and would do so. Smith thought that Congress "in the
End [would be] obliged to rely intirely upon the Army, who
will afterwards prescribe Law to their present Masters, and
the contest for Liberty may end in the Despotism of a General, who the Congress when more fearful may consent to
constitute a Dictator."[52]

On August 28, 1776, a letter was printed in the *Maryland
Journal* which was purported to have been written by "W.
Smith," "a member of the Council at New York." It expressed
Tory sentiments and was addressed to General Howe. Smith
immediately declared the letter to be a forgery. He did not

---

[50] *4: Amer. Arch.*, VI, 1180.

[51] William Smith to the Committee of the Provincial Congress, July 4,
1776; WS *Diary* I, 279.

[52] Diary entry, January 7, 1777; WS *Diary* II, 62.

publish a denial but privately stated "that I never wrote a Letter to Mr. Howe upon any subject whatsoever nor to any Man living in the smallest Degree similar to the Letter in the Mariland Journal—Such Affidavit I will nevertheless publish if it is necessary for the Satisfaction of my Country men."[53] Although Smith did not write the letter, it did blacken his name for some of the Patriots, the effect its unknown writer undoubtedly intended. The charge of Toryism was leveled at Smith throughout the autumn of 1776 and finally he was forced to move onto the Livingston Manor where he was afforded some degree of protection from the mob.

The move, however, did not protect him from the Council of Safety at Kingston, New York. On June 5, 1777, he received a summons to appear before that body. Smith had been forewarned about this by a member of the committee, his old friend and partner, John Morin Scott. In a letter Scott blamed John Jay for the summons and was suspicious about Jay's motives. Scott wrote: "For your political Sentiments as they regard the Liberty of the Subject I have always been a strenuous Advocate." He hoped that Smith's appearance before the committee would "turn out to be a political Farce." Scott believed that Jay was trying to ruin his reputation as a member of the committee and enhance his own power by linking Scott with the "Tory" William Smith. Scott thought that Jay had called for Smith's examination because Scott could be expected to oppose it as an insult, not only to William Smith, but to himself as well. For this reason Scott supported the motion to call his old friend for examination as a suspected Loyalist.[54] It is interesting that John Jay wanted to exile William Smith, but tried to keep Peter Van Schaack from being banished from New York. This points up an internal struggle that took place in revolutionary New York between moderates and radicals for control of the revolutionary movement. Jay and Governor Clinton were moderates, while John

53 William Smith to Ebanezer Hazard, September 14, 1776; *ibid.*, 6.
54 John Morin Scott to William Smith, June 3, 1777; *ibid.*, 152–153.

Morin Scott was one of the most radical leaders of the Sons of Liberty and William Smith had been identified with radicals such as Alexander MacDougall during the pre-revolutionary period. If Smith could be convicted of Toryism then the whole radical cause would suffer, to the advantage of the moderates.

William Smith did not support American independence and believed that Congress was destroying its own support by persisting in the measure. He thought that "many [were] in Arms & for War only to gain Security for antient Liberties and Privileges." These were his personal reasons for having supported Congress. He was sure that many men would now lay down their weapons for the same reasons.[55] He was correct insofar as the Whig-Loyalists were concerned. These were the reasons advanced by Andrew Allen, Robert Alexander, Peter Van Schaack and Daniel Dulany for their actions at the time of independence. During the period from the Declaration of Independence to his summons before the Council of Safety, William Smith became very critical of both Great Britain and Congress. He blamed both for the war, feeling that if they had compromised, Congress giving up the notion of independence and Great Britain the right to legislate for the colonies, the war could have been settled equitably. On June 7, 1777, Smith had to make a crucial decision, whether to support an independent United States or Great Britain.

The first question put to Smith by the committee was "whether I considered myself as a Subject of the Independent States of America?" His answer was unequivocally opposed to independence. "I told them that I was ever against it as destructive of the Interests of the Colonies. . . . I said that I considered myself as a Subject of King Geo: III of Great Britain and a Member of the old or British Government."[56] Even with this answer Smith was allowed to sign a parole granting him permission to live within the Livingston Manor,

[55] Diary entry, September 30, 1776; *ibid.*, 10–11.
[56] Diary entry, June 7, 1777; *ibid.*, 154.

although John Jay wanted to banish Smith.[57] In his parole Smith pledged to "neither directly nor indirectly by Word or Deed oppose or contravene the Measures of the United States of America."[58] His reception by the committee had been friendly, due to his previous leadership of the Whig cause in New York. Both Jay and Scott agreed to allow Smith to study the minutes of the committee meeting "with liberty to add what [he] thought proper." Smith was then invited to dine with the Council of Safety.[59]

Scott prevailed in the Council of Safety primarily because the other members of the committee did not want to see William Smith aiding the British. He was still considered to be the most astute lawyer in New York.[60] The Council of Safety was also able to let it be rumored "that [Smith] had told the Council of Safety [he] approved of the Independency [but] did not think it proper to [take] the Oath to support it at present but would hereafter."[61] Therefore Smith's popularity and prestige with the populace of New York could be used in support of independence. To the Tories he remained a Patriot, while "to my old Whigg Friends of Rank I am represented as a Tory."[62] Smith had proof of this use of his name and reputation in January, 1778 when it was "authoritatively" rumored that he had helped to draft and had signed the new constitution of New York.[63]

When the Banishing Act was passed on June 13, 1778, Smith was again summoned to appear before the Council of

[57] Ibid., 156.

[58] Ibid., 156–157.

[59] Ibid., 155.

[60] Income from his law practice averaged £2500 per annum immediately before the Revolution, according to the Loyalist Claims Commission. The Diary and Selected Papers of Chief Justice William Smith 1784–1793. Volume I: The Diary January 24, 1784 to October 5, 1785 (ed. L. F. S. Upton; Toronto, 1963), xix. Hereafter cited as WS Diary (Upton).

[61] Diary entry, July 24, 1777; WS Diary II, 183.

[62] Ibid.

[63] Diary entry, January 16, 1778; ibid., 286.

Safety and was banished "for refusing an Oath inconsistant with my Conscience and my Honor and my Views for the best Interest of my Countrymen."[64] He was considered to be a Tory despite all he had done to promote the Whig cause in New York. With New York City in British hands and Walter Butler's raids on parts of upstate New York, the Patriots were neither in the position nor the mood to deal leniently with neutrals such as William Smith. In their beleaguered position it appeared as if all who were not strong supporters of independence must be Tories and therefore a danger to the community. Smith never, at this time or after, considered himself to be a Tory. He both sympathized with and despised the Tories. Smith believed that they felt that the only mistake England had made was in not "quickening the military Aids they desired, for the Preservation of their own Significance, Interest and Power."[65] He imputed the basest motives to the Tories who wanted to prolong the war so "that the Country might hold every Thing in Future of [the king's] Grace," and who would build new fortunes and political power "out of the forfeited Estates" of the Patriots.[66] In holding this view, it is very possible that Smith was influenced by his hatred of the DeLanceys who had been the rivals of the Livingston faction in the constant pre-revolutionary struggle for political preeminence in New York. Yet Smith could also sympathize with the predicament of the Tories who "can be safe by Nothing but a Conquest of their own Country—If America prevails . . . they must finally abandon the Continent."[67]

The question now arises as to why these men, who for the first time may truly be called Whig-Loyalists, turned their backs on their pre-1776 careers as Patriots and became Loyalists. Many Patriots were unhappy when the Declaration of

---

[64] William Smith to Philip Schuyler, July 10, 1778; Schuyler Papers, New York Public Library.

[65] Diary entry, October 15, 1776; WS Diary II, 22.

[66] Diary entry, April 15, 1777; ibid., 115.

[67] Diary entry, November 9, 1776; ibid., 39.

Independence was promulgated but finally acquiesced in the measure. In the Continental Congress itself John Jay, James Duane, Robert R. Livingston, Robert Morris and John Dickinson were all opposed to independence. Morris later signed the Declaration although "in his poor opinion it was an improper time, and that it will neither promote nor redound to the honor of America, for it has caused division when we wanted union."[68] Similar reasons compelled John Dickinson to abstain from signing the Declaration but later he, as did Jay, Duane and Livingston, acquiesced in independence. Dickinson based his objections on two premises. First, he believed that without the strong central authority provided by the king's government there was great danger of dissension among the colonies. The union of the people would be destroyed if the object of the war changed from American rights to American independence. Second, the chances of success in a war for independence were slight. Dickinson believed that Great Britain could overwhelm the colonial forces if she used all of her power and feared that Britain would do so in opposition to independence.[69]

The Whig-Loyalists, who agreed with Dickinson and Morris, had other, more compelling reasons for opposing independence, reasons which compelled them to reject the measure that Dickinson and Morris could finally agree to. William Smith, for example, feared New England greatly. During his career Smith had purchased or been granted upwards of 100,000 acres of land. Much of it was located in that part of the Province of New York which later became Vermont.[70] Because of this he was involved in various land disputes both as a land owner in the contested areas and as a lawyer. This theme recurs again and again in his *Diary* in the years before

---

[68] Robert Morris to General Reed, July 20, 1776; quoted in: Charles Janeway Stille, *The Life and Times of John Dickinson 1732–1808* (Philadelphia, 1891), 197.

[69] *Ibid.*, 193–196.

[70] WS *Diary* (Upton), xxi.

the Declaration of Independence. He feared the reduction of British control in America which, he believed, would lead to the domination of New York by New England.[71] These thoughts however did not intrude upon his actions before the Revolution when Boston was being persecuted by the British.

Most of the Whig-Loyalists believed in a balanced government for the colonies. Peter Van Schaack, for example, believed in the existence and necessity of political parties, contrary to the prevailing opinion of most Americans, because

> the Bulk of the People will be divided & espouse one or other Side—from the very Temper of Man when he gets Power he will be inclined to abuse it, especially when he is irritated by the Reflection of past Opposition. . . . But where each Party continues formidable to the other & upon an equal Footing neither will dare to attempt because neither *can* oppress.[72]

For this reason Van Schaack applauded the victory of the DeLancey faction in the election of 1769. Because of it the two political factions in New York balanced one another and led to stable government. The Whig-Loyalists believed that a balance in government was necessary because of fear of the propertyless classes.

William Smith was most alarmed at the lack of class distinctions in the New York Constitution of 1777. He first saw the plan of government on October 11, 1776, when Peter R. Livingston sent him a copy of it for his comment. His objections, which he related to Livingston, began with his concept of what government should be. Smith believed that "the essential Properties of Civil Government are Power in the Majestry to protect all the Orders who live under it . . . free from the arbitrary Exertions of a Few or the capricious Wantoness of the Multitude." His main objection to the new government

---

[71] See for example: Diary entry, February 12, 1776; WS *Diary* I, 265.
[72] Peter Van Schaack to Henry Van Schaack, January 27, 1769; Hawks Mss., Hawks Papers, New York Historical Society.

was that it would be "intirely in the Hands of the Pesantry."
The new legislature, although consisting of two houses, was
to be elected annually. To Smith the two houses should cater
to distinct classes in society, which was not provided for under the new constitution. What then was the advantage of a
two-house legislature? "Unless the Law givers are a Compound of distinct Classes of Men really as well as nominally,
they will have but one Spirit and can therefore neither check
nor aid each other." Smith also believed that it was dangerous
"to admit Persons with very small Property" to a share in
government. He considered it to be hardly equitable for a
propertyless man to have an equal voice in government with
a wealthy individual. "The poor being the Majority ought not
to refuse a security to others against the Spoil of their Property
—They lose Nothing by being obliged to elect Men of Sub-
stance attached to the Territory."[73]

William Smith, even while an ardent Patriot, had no objection to, indeed he had a preference for, the control of
New York affairs by the landed aristocracy of the colony. The
origins of the Whig Party in New York were not based on any
degree of class struggle. The Livingston group as well as the
Tory, or DeLancey, faction was made up of oligarchs. The
struggle between the two parties was basically which upper
class group would control the government. Smith and the
other Whig-Loyalists were opposed primarily to the extension
of power by the British government over colonial affairs. They
wanted no interference from Parliament in the local oligarchical control of the colonies.

The great difference between the Whig-Loyalists and the
Tories and Whigs lay in their concept of the British empire.
To the Tories, such as Thomas Hutchinson, any idea of local
autonomy for the colonies was abhorrent. In 1769 Hutchinson
wrote that New York was "in full expectation of an American
Parliament" and ridiculed the idea because it tended to lessen

---

[73] Diary entry, October 14, 1776; WS *Diary* II, 18.

the supremacy of royal authority.[74] Hutchinson had however supported Franklin's Albany Plan in 1754, but this plan would not have lessened royal authority. The Albany Conference had in fact been called by the home government in an attempt to strengthen colonial opposition to the French.

The political ideology of the Whigs, from the time of the Stamp Act, was based on the ideas of John Locke as expressed in *An Essay Concerning the True Original, Extent and End of Civil Government.* The Whig-Loyalists held to his theories with the same fervor as did the ardent revolutionaries for, as Carl Becker pointed out, "most Americans had absorbed Locke's works as a kind of political gospel."[75] Locke wrote that reason, the only sure guide given to men by God, is the only foundation for just government. Reasonable governments derive their just powers only from the consent of the governed. All of the Whig-Loyalists accepted these theories. They also accepted the compact theory of government which is pre-supposed by Locke. As Peter Van Schaack put it:

> The only foundation of all legitimate governments, is certainly a compact between the rulers and the people, containing mutual conditions, and equally obligatory on both the contracting parties.[76]

Daniel Dulany had cited Locke as early as the time of the Stamp Act. The contract theory is implicit in *Considerations*:

> [The colonists] entered into a compact with the crown. . . . By these charters, founded upon the unalienable rights of the subject, and upon the most sacred compact, the colonies claim a right of exemption from taxes *not imposed with their* consent.—They claim it upon . . . principles on which their compact with the crown was originally founded.[77]

---

[74] Thomas Hutchinson to Francis Bernard, October 27, 1769; in: Diary entry, August 12, 1775; WS *Diary* I, 235.

[75] Becker, *Declaration of Independence,* 27.

[76] Diary entry, January, 1776; Van Schaack, *Peter Van Schaack,* 54.

[77] Dulany, *Considerations,* 634.

The Whig-Loyalists also believed that resistance to unjust government was lawful "in cases of gross and palpable infractions on the part of the governing power."[78] William Smith thereby declared that the colonies were justified in resisting the Intolerable Acts since they were promulgated "to inforce the Claim of absolute Supremacy." The colonists were "driven to the alternative of open Violence, or an unconditional Submission."[79] Under the compact as it existed between Great Britain and her colonies there was no provision for arbitration by an "Impartial Judge. . . . Their Controversies are therefore to be decided by Negotiation and Treaty, or on an Appeal to the Lord of Hosts by Battle; for neither is obliged to surrender its essential Rights at the Will of the other; & each may lawfully exert its own self-preserving Powers."[80]

It is difficult to ascertain the reasons why Dr. Benjamin Church became a Loyalist and a spy. It is probable that he did so for similar reasons to those of the other Whig-Loyalists. According to Allen French however he became a spy because of the money he was paid. Church lived beyond his means and maintained a mistress. The money that Gage paid him helped to support this establishment.[81] Yet this does not tell the whole or even part of the story for Dr. Church was very selective in the material he passed on to General Gage. For example, although he signed Benedict Arnold's commission for the attack on Fort Ticonderoga he did not forward this information to Gage despite the fact that he was in correspondence with the general at the time. A careful reading of all of the letters attributed to Church reveals that he did not pass any urgent information, but merely informed Gage of general trends of thought in the rebel camp. When he passed on military information he constantly overestimated

---

[78] Van Schaack, *Peter Van Schaack*, 54.

[79] "My thoughts as a Rule for my own Conduct," diary entry, June 9, 1776; *WS Diary* I, 274.

[80] *Ibid.*, 272.

[81] French, *General Gage's Informers*, 149 *passim*.

the strength of the American positions, although he was in an excellent position to obtain detailed accurate knowledge.[82] It seems as if all of his letters to Gage in 1775 were designed to induce the British commander to break off hostilities and find a peaceful solution to the crisis before the colonies decided to declare independence. In the letter which Gage received on May 24, 1775 Church wrote:

> Should hostilities be long continued & the present demands insisted upon I am fearfull of the event [independence], may I never see the day when I shall not dare to call myself a British American.[83]

His reasoning seems to be similar to that of William Smith, for Church also believed that colonial resistance to Great Britain was justified. He opposed all of the Parliamentary attempts to legislate for the colonies and wrote:

> Numberless have been the attacks made upon our free constitution; numberless the grievances we now resent: but the Hydra mischief, is the violation on my right, as a British American freeholder, in not being consulted in framing those statutes I am required to obey. . . .
> The state is only free, where the people are governed by laws which they have a share in making; and that country is totally enslaved, where one single law can be made or repealed, without the interposition or consent of the people.[84]

The Whig-Loyalists broke with the Patriots only over the question of independence. And although they separated from the Patriots, they retained their belief in John Locke and the compact theory of government. Applying this theory to the British empire, William Smith noted that the contract between the mother country and her colonies bound England

---

82 *Ibid.*
83 *Ibid.*, 156–157.
84 Vaughan (ed.), *Chronicles*, 39–40.

to protect and promote the Colonies, according to the good
Faith inspired by the Grants and Charters and other royal
and National Acts in their Favor, consistant with the Weal
of both Countries; And it obliged the Plantations to submit
to her Authority in all Cases not repugnant to their Grants,
Charters and established Privileges; and to contribute to
the common Felicity and Defense of the Empire.[85]

The break came only over the Declaration of Independence.
The theories expressed above by William Smith, Daniel Dulany and Peter Van Schaack agree very closely with the first
paragraph of the Declaration where Thomas Jefferson wrote
that

> Governments are instituted among Men, deriving their just
> powers from the consent of the governed, That whenever
> any Form of Government becomes destructive of these ends,
> it is the Right of the People to alter or abolish it.[86]

Jefferson went on to state that the political contract binding
the colonies to the mother country had been broken and therefore "these United Colonies are, and of Right ought to be free
and Independent States."[87]

This statement found the Whig-Loyalists in disagreement
with the Patriots. They believed that Great Britain was almost
entirely blameable for the war but, as William Smith stated,
"Neither of the contracting Parties may dissolve this Compact,
as long as their joint Aim in the union, to wit their mutual
Prosperity, can be attained by it."[88] Therefore, "when Terms
are proposed, consistant with the original Compact, neither
Party can reject them and be innocent."[89] This was the focal
point of the argument for William Smith. He believed that

---

[85] *WS Diary* I, 272.
[86] *E. H. D.*, IX, 877.
[87] *Ibid.*, 879.
[88] *WS Diary* I, 272.
[89] *Ibid.*, 277.

neither party had fulfilled this obligation but, since the contract had been promulgated for the "mutual prosperity" of the empire, it had not been dissolved. Both Great Britain and the American colonies still had something to gain from the union of the empire. To William Smith it would have been extremely difficult for the contract to be broken. Although he believed that tyranny should be opposed and tyrants deposed, the state should survive both the tyrant and the tyranny. As early as 1753 he, in *The Independent Reflector,* stated that "rather than live without Law, without Society, and the innumerable Blessings it includes, better it would be, to suffer with only a distant Hope of Redress, the ungoverned Sway of the most arbitrary Monarch the World ever saw."[90]

Peter Van Schaack was willing to concede that the contract might possibly have been dissolved in 1776, but believed that each individual person could only be released from his allegiance by his own conscience. This was "a Question of Morality as well as of Religion in which every Man must judge, as he must answer, for himself. . . . He can never be justifiable in the Sight of God or Man if he acts against the Light of his own Conviction." This belief coincided closely with the Lockean theory of compact governments. If the compact had been dissolved as the Declaration of Independence supposed, then "we must have been reduced to a State of Nature, in which the Powers of Government reverted to, as they originated from, the People." Since man was "by Nature *free, equal* & independent," upon the dissolution of the compact he now regained "that Portion of his natural Liberty which each Individual had before surrendered to the Government . . . and to which no one Society could make any Claim until he *incorporated* himself in it."[91] Van Schaack thereby believed that first one had to answer the question of whether or not the compact had been dissolved. If so, man, being in a state of nature, had to decide

---

[90] *Independent Reflector,* 338.

[91] Peter Van Schaack to the Albany Committee of Safety, January 25, 1777; Peter Van Schaack Papers, New York Historical Society.

for himself to what government he would give his allegiance. It could not be automatically assumed that the government of the independent United States claimed the allegiance of all the denizens of the thirteen rebelling colonies.

Since the Whig-Loyalists rejected the Declaration of Independence, yet believed resistance to England to be justified, we must now ask: What sort of a government should thus be established for the colonies? This question must be answered by Peter Van Schaack and William Smith who were the only Whig-Loyalists to set their thoughts down on paper in a full and explicit manner. The beliefs of the other Whig-Loyalists can only be gleaned from short, nonexplanatory statements in their letters. John Locke himself asked not what powers a government had in fact, but what authority it ought to have, authority to which men would willingly consent. William Smith, following this part of Lockean thought, conceived of the British constitution as a set of doctrines which could, and should, be adapted to meet the needs of a growing empire. The British constitution had been established long before the colonies had been discovered. For Smith "the Question therefore is not, what the Constitution was, but what, present Circumstances considered, it ought to be."[92] Smith wrote these "Thoughts upon the Dispute between Great Britain and her Colonies" soon after the passage of the Stamp Act, but his theory of empire remained constant throughout the revolution-

---

[92] William Smith, "Thoughts upon the Dispute between Great Britain and her Colonies," in Robert M. Calhoon, "William Smith Jr's. Alternative to the American Revolution," *William and Mary Quarterly,* 3rd series, XXII, 1965, 105–118, 113. Hereafter cited as WS "Thoughts." Although Smith wrote these "Thoughts" during the period from 1765–1767, during the Stamp Act crisis and its aftermath, his diary for the years 1775–1776 testifies to his unswerving commitment to these earlier ideas. They are therefore presented at this point. It should be particularly noted that Smith's detailed constitutionalism was a strong force pulling him away from the Whigs in the immediate pre-independence years.

ary era. In his "Observations on America," written in 1785, he expressed much the same view of the empire.[93]

William Smith believed that the structure of the empire was a contributing factor to the conflicting views of American rights and obligations held by political leaders on both sides of the Atlantic. Since he conceived of the constitution, structurally, as an organic, changing institution, Smith assumed that changes in the structure of the empire would create a more stable and harmonious union which would be beneficial to all its parts. Although Great Britain was blameable for the war and should be judged accordingly, Smith believed that ultimate guilt lay with those men, be they English or American, who wanted to dismember the empire, for it could be beneficial to all.[94] He believed that the compact had not been broken but could be revised due to its organic nature.

The Whig-Loyalists believed that the Empire was linked together by indissoluble bonds. William Samuel Johnson's long stay in England strengthened and deepened his appreciation of the value of the common heritage that England and America shared. This common tradition was strengthened for Johnson by the mutual economic interests that tied the two areas together. Severance of these ties, through American independence, would bring distress upon all parts of the Empire.[95] Peter Van Schaack thought in much the same way. He believed that there was a point at which the empire as a whole must take precedence over its individual parts. As he put it: "every *individual* part must give way to the *general good*."[96] William Smith wrote that the colonies were established by Parliament and were therefore national establishments and under Parliamentary control. [97] Although the colonies claimed some degree

---

[93] "William Smith's 'Observations on America'," (ed. Oscar Zeichner) *New York History*, XXIII, 1942, 328–340.

[94] WS *Diary* I, 271–277.

[95] Groce, *William Samuel Johnson*, 90.

[96] Diary entry, January, 1776; Van Schaack, *Peter Van Schaack*, 55.

[97] WS *Diary* I, 271–272.

of exemption from this control, they recognized "at the same
Time, the Supremacy of Great Britain."[98] Smith also believed
that although Great Britain was supreme, she could not take
any action which would detract from "the common Safety of
the whole Body," and that the various branches of the empire
had to be consulted as to matters of common defense and interest.[99] These bonds which tied the Empire together were,
the Whig-Loyalists believed, "conducive of the general prosperity of the Empire."[100]

The Whig-Loyalists thought in terms of a doctrine of a
decentralized empire in which each part would have some
share of the responsibility of the whole. Daniel Dulany expressed this concept in *Considerations*.[101] He believed that
each part of the empire was subject only to the general over-
sight of the king and Parliament. Each part of the empire
organized and controlled its own internal affairs, but matters
which concerned the empire as a whole were to be subject to
Parliamentary control. He considered Parliament to be supreme. William Samuel Johnson seems to have had much the
same idea when he expressed a preference for "Home Rule"
with the "supreme power" over the empire lodged in Parliament.[102] William Smith believed Parliament should enjoy as
much supremacy as was "not incompatible with the Common
Felicity of the Empire."[103] To Smith this meant that the colonies should have the liberty to dispose of their own property,
meaning that they should have some say in matters of taxation
and legislation.[104]

The question of what degree of subordination America owed

[98] WS "Thoughts", 117.

[99] Plan for peace drawn up by William Smith for Thomas Smith and
John Morin Scott, November 25, 1775; WS *Diary* I, 246.

[100] William Smith to the Committee of the Provincial Congress, July
4, 1776; *ibid.*, 280.

[101] See above, Chapter 2.

[102] William Samuel Johnson to Nathaniel Rogers, November 15, 1769;
William Samuel Johnson Papers, Connecticut Historical Society.

[103] WS *Diary* I, 274.

[104] Diary entry, September 28, 1776; WS *Diary* II, 7.

to the British Parliament was taken up by Peter Van Schaack. In answering this question he believed it was necessary to disregard "the principles of Mr. Locke and other advocates for the rights of mankind, as little to the purpose." Van Schaack believed that a supreme power was necessary in every state, but "at the same time I foresee the destructive consequences of a right in Parliament to bind us in all cases whatsoever." Since the British constitution was in many respects beneficial to the colonies, they "derive advantage even from some kind of subordination." Without some degree of control by Parliament, Van Schaack felt the colonies would descend into "anarchy and confusion." He therefore desired to see a constitution promulgated which would find "some middle way" out of the difficulties created by the Revolution. In his estimation the benefits of a supreme power would be preserved "while the abuses of that power to the prejudice of the colonists, should be guarded against." This, he hoped, would be the effect of the American Revolution.[105]

William Smith was the only one of the Whig-Loyalists to write about his theories of government in an explicit manner. Several times over a span of twenty years he wrote out his ideas concerning the government of the British empire. Taken together they form a clear expression of the Whig-Loyalist concept of government, for I believe that men such as Peter Van Schaack, Daniel Dulany and William Samuel Johnson, not to mention the others, would have agreed with William Smith's political ideology. Basic to Smith's plan of government was the idea of an American Parliament. This he considered to be the best solution to the problem of holding the empire together.[106] It was for this reason that William Smith had such great hopes for the Continental Congress in 1774 and 1775. It is apparent that he believed it would become the basis

---

[105] Diary entry, January, 1776; Van Schaack, *Peter Van Schaack,* 54–58.

[106] William Smith to Philip Schuyler, July 23, 1774; Schuyler Papers, New York Public Library.

of legislative unity in the colonies. But Smith did not want this Parliament to supersede the colonial assemblies. The assemblies were, in his plan, to elect the delegates to the House of Commons of the American Parliament, just as the Assemblies of many of the colonies appointed the delegates to Congress. In this way "we shall collect the Wisdom of the whole Continent, and find the Members acting upon Principles . . . and with a Liberality unbiassed by the partial Prejudices, prevalent in the little Districts by which they were sent." He also desired the new constitution to set up "a Lord Lieutenant as in Ireland, and a Council . . . appointed by the crown" on which the best minds of America (William Smith included) would sit. The Council was in keeping with Smith's notions about the separation of powers. The House of Commons was to represent the colonial assemblies, therefore the Council should represent men of property and; as a safeguard against corruption, be appointed for life. Executive power was to be vested in the office of lord lieutenant. The crown would retain the veto it held over colonial legislation "and the British Parliament its Legislative Supremacy, in *all cases* relative to *Life, Liberty and Property*, except in the Matter of Taxation for *general Aids*, or the immediate, internal support of the American Government."[107] In some respects this plan is similar to Joseph Galloway's plan of 1774, but was delineated before Galloway wrote.

To William Smith, as to almost every other American in the revolutionary period, the British policy of colonial taxation was the basis for the American Revolution. His plan of government attempted to solve this problem through the creation of an American Parliament. No taxes were to be raised without the consent of this legislature. It was to vote the amount necessary for the safety of the empire and settle "the Quotas of each Colony & to force a Defaulting Province." Each colonial assembly was to collect its quota in whatever manner it thought

---

[107] WS "Thoughts," 114–116.

proper.[108] The American Parliament was assured of its right to assemble for "as often as Great Britain shall renew her Requisitions for the Contributions of the Colonies . . . it shall be lawful for them to hold Congresses." The Americans were to receive a further guarantee in that Great Britain was expected to account for the disposition of the American taxes, "shewing that it has been entirely expended for the support of the Navy & Army and other National Purposes of Defense."[109]

Unlike the matter of taxation, William Smith accepted the necessity of the supremacy of Great Britain in the regulation of commerce.[110] But the money raised by this form of indirect taxation, incidental revenue proceeding from commercial regulation, was to be expended solely for the defense of the empire.[111] As in the case of taxation, the money was either to pass directly into the colonial treasuries or, if collected in England, was to be credited to the colonies.[112] The American Parliament was to receive an accounting of how the money was spent.[113]

Freedom of religion was another matter that Smith thought crucial to the well being of America. He was deeply concerned lest Great Britain try to impose an Anglican establishment upon the colonies. The new constitution promulgated by his plan of government would guarantee that all matters concerning religion would be left to the judgment of the colonial assemblies.[114]

William Smith's plan of government for the colonies is remarkably similar in some respects to the Durham Report of

---

[108] William Smith to Philip Schuyler, May 16, 1775; Schuyler Papers, New York Public Library.

[109] Plan for Peace. . . , November 25, 1775; WS *Diary* I, 246.

[110] WS "Thoughts," 117.

[111] Plan for peace. . . , WS *Diary* I, 246.

[112] William Smith to Philip Schuyler, May 16, 1775; Schuyler Papers, New York Public Library.

[113] Plan for peace. . . , WS *Diary* I, 246.

[114] William Smith to Philip Schuyler, May 16, 1775; Schuyler Papers, New York Public Library.

1839 and the British North America Act of 1867. It is probable that Smith, as Chief Justice of Quebec,[115] was influential in the formation of Lord Dorchester's ideas on government, and through Dorchester the subsequent proceedings concerning the establishment of the British Commonwealth of Nations.[116] Many of Smith's ideas and recommendations reappear in the Durham Report. Thus William Smith's plan of government for the colonies did constitute a practical attempt to regulate the relationship of Great Britain and her American colonies. He was sure that if his "Simple Proposal" was adopted, peace and prosperity would be the result, "for the whole System of our Grievances will then fall like Scaffolds to a building reared and finished."[117] The American Parliament would be able to discuss grievances, and the colonial guarantees promulgated by the new constitution would lead to "the Establishment of a compleat and permanent Harmony between all the Branches of the Empire."[118]

> But the Capital Advantages of this Scheme, will be the Recovery of the Colonies, to a firmer Confidence in the *Justice* and *Affection* of the Parent State. And by opening to her the Conduits of sure, full and constant Information, enabling her so to regulate and improve this vast, dependent, growing Territory, as to unite every Branch of Empire, by the Cords of Love and Interest, and give Peace, Health and Vigor to the whole.[119]

The chief problem presented by Smith's plan of government was of course that while it was more liberal than Joseph Galloway's plan of union, it gave Great Britain more authority than

---

115 See below, Chapter 7.

116 For Smith's influence see: Hilda M. Neatby, "Chief Justice William Smith: an 18th Century Whig Imperialist," *Canadian Historical Review*, XXVIII, 1947, 44–67.

117 William Smith to Philip Schuyler, May 16, 1775; Schuyler Papers, New York Public Library.

118 Plan for peace. . . , *WS Diary* I, 246.

119 WS "Thoughts," 116.

most Patriots were willing to allow in 1774–1776. Galloway's plan provided for the creation of a "British American Legislature" which was to constitute "an inferior and distant branch of the British legislature, united and incorporated with it."[120] This plan was unacceptable to Congress. There is no reason to assume that Smith's plan, had it been presented, would have been any more successful, despite the fact that it provided for more American autonomy. The Whig-Loyalist view of empire was more liberal than the Tory view, but was more conservative than the Patriot conception. By 1774 men like John Adams were unwilling to accept any limitations on American liberty. As Patrick Henry put it in the course of debate on the Galloway plan of union: If Congress was to accept the plan "We shall liberate our constituents from a corrupt House of Commons, but throw them into the arms of an American legislature, that may be bribed by that nation which avows, in the face of the world, that bribery is part of her system of government. Before we are obliged to pay taxes as they do, let us be as free as they; let us have our trade open with all the world."[121]

The Whig-Loyalists disliked the idea of an aristocratic, centralized empire of the kind Galloway proposed as much as did the Patriots. They differed with men like Adams and Henry in that they conceived of the British empire as a tangible community beneficial to all its parts. They were willing to accept some restrictions upon American liberty to maintain the existence of the community; the Patriots were not.

---

[120] Debate on the Galloway plan of union ([28 September] 1774), *E. H. D.*, IX, 810. The Galloway plan of union (28 September 1774), *ibid.*, 812.

[121] *Ibid.*, 810.

7

A REBIRTH OF LEADERSHIP

The roles that the Whig-Loyalists, as they may now be called in fact, played during the course of the American Revolution varied. Daniel Dulany and William Samuel Johnson, having remained in rebel-held territory, were relatively passive during the war years. Daniel Leonard and Peter Van Schaack sat out the conflict in England as did many other Loyalists. Dr. Benjamin Church died soon after his release and exchange in 1778 and William Byrd III had committed suicide in 1777. But Robert Alexander, Andrew Allen and William Smith took active parts in the struggle, doing all in their power within Loyalist ranks to prevent the emergence of a national American state. At times, however, they were mistrusted by the Tories. No wonder, since these three men were the most active of the Whig-Loyalists in the Patriot cause, especially in the two years before the Declaration of Independence.

Daniel Dulany remained in Maryland throughout the war, but never took an oath of allegiance to the revolutionary government. From his legalistic outlook, the proprietary government remained the only legitimate governing body in Maryland. Dulany refused to extend personal *de jure* recognition to the actual government of the Maryland Convention but gave it *de facto* status. He came to terms with the government by staying neutral, becoming a passive Loyalist.

Dulany was a valuable asset to the revolutionary cause in Maryland due to his neutrality. His name was still influential in the colonies and the fact that he remained in Maryland could be used with good effect to keep others who admired him from becoming active Loyalists. Even so, the war years were not easy ones for Daniel Dulany. In February, 1777 the Baltimore Town Whig Club, acting under a policy of ridding Maryland of nonsupporters, ordered Dulany and his family "to leave Town immediately, and the Province within three days, or their Lives should answer for their refusal."[1] This threat however was immediately nullified by the state Assembly. They realized that if Dulany actively used his formidable talents for the benefit of the Loyalist cause he would be a much greater danger than he was while living in retirement on his estate. He was therefore allowed to remain in Baltimore County even though he refused to take an oath of fidelity to the independent state of Maryland and forfeited his civil rights. Dulany was disbarred from the legal profession and his property was subjected to triple taxation. This last measure was not to prove a hardship until 1781 when the taxes were collected for the first time. None of Dulany's land or property was ever confiscated because of his loyalty to the crown, but in the years before the outbreak of the Revolution he had given title to a large part of his estate to his sons. As they became Loyalists, this property was confiscated and the Dulany family lost about one-half of its combined wealth before the end of the war.

Much like Dulany, William Samuel Johnson remained in Connecticut during the Revolution despite the fact that he was a known Loyalist. After the adoption of the Declaration of Independence Johnson retired from the Connecticut Council and lived in Stratford. He had considerable freedom of move-

---

[1] William Eddis to Robert Eden, July 23, 1777; Land, *Dulanys of Maryland*, 321.

ment within the colony and continued to practice law until
November, 1777. In that month attorneys were required to
subscribe to an oath of allegiance to Connecticut as a "free and
independent State."[2] Johnson, as has been noted, refused and
was compelled to give up his practice. He retained his freedom
however and for a time was careful to do nothing that would
give offense to the revolutionary authorities, but he became
"very unhappy with the insults of the common people."[3]

The town of Stratford had enjoyed close commercial relations with New York City prior to the Revolution and the
subsequent British occupation of the city. The prosperity of
the town depended upon trade with New York. Since New
York City was under British control, Stratford suffered some
loss of prosperity during the war and carried on an illicit trade
with the English and Loyalists on Long Island. Because of this
illegal commercial activity, many Stratford residents developed
Loyalist, or non-patriotic, sympathies. Many Tory plots were
rumored to have originated in Stratford. A town meeting did
nothing to lessen the suspicion with which Stratford was
viewed by the Patriots when it voted to remit the fines of local
soldiers who had deserted from the Continental Army. It was
during the development of this climate of opinion that Loyalist
irregular forces, operating from Long Island, began to stage
raids along the Connecticut coastline, burning villages and
farms.[4]

These raiding expeditions caused a degree of panic in Stratford and William Samuel Johnson, as an acquaintance of
General Tryon's was requested in a petition to use his influence with the British to save the town from being burned.[5]
Johnson, in order to protect himself, drafted a paper by which
the inhabitants of Stratford promised to protect him from

---

[2] Groce, *William Samuel Johnson*, 106.

[3] Samuel B. Webb to Mrs. Simpson, August 9, 1778; *ibid.*, 107.

[4] See below. Robert Alexander played a role in this warfare.

[5] Petition, July 12, 1779; William Samuel Johnson Papers, Connecticut
Historical Society.

"Insult, Injury or abuse" if he wrote to Tyron.[6] According to one of the more patriotic residents of Stratford, Johnson was willing to contact Tryon, but recommended "that Independency must [be] given up as the Preliminary."[7]

Johnson's activities immediately came to the attention of the revolutionary authorities. Upon being informed of what appeared to be treasonable action on the part of the former Councilman, Major General Oliver Wolcott sent Lieutenant Colonel Jonathan Dimon to investigate. Wolcott, of the Continental Army, was charged with defending Connecticut from the raids staged by Tryon and the Loyalists. His aide, Dimon, upon arrival in Stratford, discovered that no correspondence with Tryon had actually begun, although William Samuel Johnson admitted to having contemplated such action. He therefore recommended Johnson's arrest as a traitor.[8] Wolcott ordered Dimon to arrest Johnson and turn him over to the civilian Selectmen of Farmington where he was to be placed under restraint "to prevent his having Any Correspondence with the Enemy."[9]

William Samuel Johnson was very fortunate that the Continental Army, as represented by Oliver Wolcott and Jonathan Dimon, was not in a position to decide his fate. From the tone of the general's communications touching on the matter it appears as if he would have incarcerated Johnson in the Simsbury salt mines where other Loyalists considered to be a threat to the United States had been jailed. However Johnson's case was turned over to the Connecticut Council of Safety and Governor Trumbull. These men were all old friends of Johnson's and had been his political cronies during the pre-revolutionary era. At his trial Johnson pointed out that in offering to

---

[6] Groce, *William Samuel Johnson*, 109.

[7] N. Wetmore to Governor Jonathan Trumbull, July 9, 1779; William Samuel Johnson Papers, Connecticut Historical Society.

[8] Lt. Col. Jonathan Dimon to Maj. Gen. Oliver Wolcott, July 17, 1779; *ibid.*

[9] Maj. Gen. Oliver Wolcott to Lt. Col. Jonathan Dimon, July 18, 1779; *ibid.*

correspond with the British he had only agreed to a petition put forth by the people of Stratford. No letters had actually been exchanged with Tryon.[10] He then, to avoid being jailed, took an oath of allegiance to the independent state of Connecticut The Council of Safety

> *having long been convinced of the Integrity and Upright-ness of the said Dr. Johnson, and being fully* satisfied that Dr. Johnson's word and Oath may be relied upon, *and that his future Residence with his Family will be consistent with the Safety of the State,* do humbly advise his Excellency the Governor to permit [?] the said Dr. William Samuel Johnson to return to his family—'till further Orders—[11]

Governor Trumbull accepted the advice of the Council of Safety and Johnson was allowed to return to Stratford.

This episode constituted William Samuel Johnson's sole attempt to sway the course of events during the Revolution. Upon his return to Stratford he was allowed to resume his law practice, having taken the required oath of allegiance. As a mark of the esteem with which he was held in the state, despite his loyalism, is the fact that during the August, 1779 term of the Superior Court of Connecticut he handled no less than twenty-nine cases.[12] But it is apparent that he was no longer fully trusted by Governor Trumbull, who ordered the Stratford authorities to keep Johnson under surveillance. If the safety of the town called for measures to be taken against William Samuel Johnson, Trumbull was to be notified.[13]

Daniel Leonard and Peter Van Schaack were also inactive during the war but they, for reasons already discussed, became

---

[10] Groce, *William Samuel Johnson,* 110.

[11] Legislative Council and Council of Safety, July 28, 1779; William Samuel Johnson Papers, Connecticut Historical Society.

[12] Groce, *William Samuel Johnson,* 111.

[13] Greene, "William Samuel Johnson and the American Revolution," 175.

residents of the British Isles. Leonard was to remain completely inactive. When the British evacuated Boston he sailed to Halifax with the fleet and then to England when the army went to New York. After the Declaration of Independence was promulgated Leonard's property was confiscated by Massachusetts and he was proscribed. He was forbidden to set foot on Massachusetts soil under penalty of death. Leonard has left us no correspondence for the war years and his biographers have discovered little about his life during the period. His behavior was probably similar to that of Peter Van Schaack.

Peter Van Schaack supported himself in London with the interest earned on money invested there in the names of his children.[14] He occupied himself with frequent attendance at sessions of the House of Commons, especially when American affairs were debated, and in having his eyes cared for. Van Schaack was able to bear the expense of living in London although many Loyalists, having escaped from America with little but their lives, were not. As a lawyer he therefore aided these less fortunate exiles in obtaining remuneration from the British government for their losses. He served in that capacity without accepting compensation.[15]

Three of the Whig-Loyalists became extremely active partisans in the British effort to subdue the revolting colonies after they had made the critical decision to cast their lot with England. However, Robert Alexander was the only one to become active militarily. Alexander seems to have suffered misgivings about having left Maryland with General Howe in September, 1777. In June, 1778 he wrote to his former friend, Governor Thomas Johnson of Maryland, asking permission to return to his home "from motives which your own feelings will readily suggest, but Prudence forbids me to take this step without some assurance of my personal safety. You well know my sentiments and Conduct in the Publick Affairs of America,

---

[14] American Loyalists, Commission of Enquiry, II, 126–127.
[15] Van Schaack, *Peter Van Schaack*, 165.

and appealing to him, who is the Searcher of all Hearts, I can with Truth affirm, I still retain the same Opinion." He asked for terms upon which he could return, stating he would "most readily embrace them, and return immediately to Country, Family and Friends."[16] There is no record of any reply to this appeal. If there was one, the answer was unsatisfactory to Alexander, for he remained in New York City. In May, 1780 he was outlawed for high treason by the General Court of the Western Shore of Maryland.[17] Five months later, two-thirds of his real estate and one-half of his slaves were confiscated. The remainder of his property was left to the use of his family who were forced to pay triple taxes until the end of the war. His wife was allowed six slaves for her personal use and a house with garden, not to exceed thirty acres. Altogether 860 acres were sold by the state and 430 acres were left for the use of his family.[18]

During the British occupation of New York City guerilla warfare was carried out by both rebel and Loyalist paramilitary forces in an area of no-man's land ringing the city. This territory encompassed southwestern Connecticut, Westchester County, The Bronx, northeastern New Jersey, the Long Island Sound and the Lower Bay of New York harbor. Although the "better elements" on both sides condemned and attempted to suppress these irregular forces, raids were conducted throughout the war years. The purposes of the guerilla warfare were varied. Food was obtained, enemy supplies were decreased, information was gathered, prisoners were taken for use in exchanges, and in general, the opposition was harried in every conceivable fashion.

As a result of this warfare, Governor William Franklin of New Jersey, Robert Alexander of Maryland, and Governor

---

[16] Robert Alexander to Governor Thomas Johnson, June 22, 1778; *Archives of Maryland: Journal and Correspondence of the Council of Maryland, April 1, 1778–October 26, 1779* (ed. William Hand Browne; XXI, Baltimore, 1901), 146.

[17] Proclamation printed in *Maryland History Magazine*, IV, 287–288.

[18] American Loyalists, Commission of Enquiry, XXXVI, 161, 181.

William Tryon of New York proposed that a Loyalist militia unit be formed to defend the outlying areas which were being attacked by the rebels. Sir Henry Clinton, acting on the advice of William Smith, agreed to the proposal and in November, 1780 the organization known as the Associated Loyalists was formally recognized by the government as an independent corporate armed force serving the British crown. William Franklin was installed as president and Robert Alexander as a member of the board of directors.

The creation of this organization, instead of solving the problem of guerilla warfare around New York, magnified it. Under the leadership of the board of directors the Associated Loyalists raised the art of plundering to new heights. They were extremely brutal and were dreaded more by the patriotic inhabitants of New Jersey and Connecticut than any other Loyalist force. The board of directors, although they did not themselves lead troops, seem to have used their private army for purposes of revenge, even going so far as to authorize the hanging of a Continental Army captain in retaliation for the execution of a captured Associator.[19]

William Smith's role in the war was far more "gentlemanly" than was Robert Alexander's. The fact that William Smith had become a Loyalist was a great coup for the British. Two Loyalist secret agents, Paul Wentworth of New Hampshire and John Vardill of New York (a close friend of Peter Van Schaack's), both recommended that the British attempt to win Smith over early in the war. Vardill believed that Smith had "more influence over the rebels in the province [of New York] than any other person."[20] Wentworth wrote that few men were as able as William Smith. He would be a tremendous asset to the British cause "if he could be trusted."[21] As we

---

[19] William Allen Benton, "New York City, A Loyalist Stronghold, 1775–1783" (Unpublished M. A. thesis, Lehigh University, 1962), 12–16.

[20] Carl Van Doren, *Secret History of the American Revolution* (New York, 1941), 75.

[21] *Ibid.*, 77.

know, Smith did join the British in New York City, but there is no evidence of any active attempts at recruitment on the part of the British or Loyalists. Wentworth's remarks take on a curious significance when we examine Smith's career in Loyalist New York. He seems never to have completely lost the trust of the rebels and was one of only three prominent New York Loyalists whose property was never confiscated.[22] Peter Van Schaack was another.

William Smith never found favor with the Tories, who distrusted his motives in coming to New York City. Remembering Smith's intense partisanship in the decades preceeding the war, Judge Thomas Jones and other Tories would not confide in William Smith. Jones claimed that Smith had never signed an oath of allegiance to the independent State of New York solely because by his refusal he could remain on the Royal Council and spy for the rebels. According to Jones, Smith had come to New York, not from any sense of loyalty to the crown, but for the sole purpose of spying on the Tories.[23] Smith did, however, find favor with the English. He favorably impressed the Carlisle Commission, which was attempting to negotiate a compromise peace along much the same lines as Smith had proposed some years earlier. As a result he was appointed Chief Justice of New York in 1779, joined Sir Henry Clinton's staff as an intelligence officer, and became a member of the New York Council.[24] The fact that Smith was never trusted by the Tories can, in part, be attributed to his own actions at this time. With Sir Henry Clinton's knowledge, Smith maintained his correspondence with friends in revolutionary New York, including George Clinton, governor of the state.[25]

William Smith's actions as a Loyalist, although distrusted by the Tories, were consistent with his political philosophy as ex-

---

[22] WS *Diary* (Upton), xxi.
[23] Jones, *New York during the Revolutionary War*, I, 44–46, 59, 144–153.
[24] WS *Diary* (Upton), xxiii.
[25] WS *Diary* I, 7–8.

pressed throughout the era. As he wrote in his *Diary*, he tried
to "persevere nevertheless in what [I] conceive to be the true
Interests of the whole Empire & if possible bring on an American Parliament."[26]

In his capacity as an intelligence officer for Sir Henry
Clinton, Smith had a curious involvement with two notable
Americans of the era, Benedict Arnold and Ethan Allen. William Smith's contacts with Arnold began during the early stages
of the West Point commandant's negotiations with Clinton.
Smith was completely trusted by Sir Henry and took part in
the Arnold affair from the very beginning. It was perhaps more
than a coincidence that Arnold used Joshua Hett Smith's house
for his meetings with Major John Andre. Joshua Hett Smith
was William Smith's youngest brother and a Patriot. Much of
Arnold's correspondence with Major Andre, Beverley Robinson
and Sir Henry Clinton was addressed to William Smith for
transmittal to them and Smith read and advised on these
letters.[27] Smith was hopeful that Benedict Arnold's betrayal
would be only the first of many desertions from the American
cause and believed that George Washington hated Arnold
solely because Arnold had done what he, Washington, had
intended to do. Smith based this supposition on a conversation
he had had with Dr. John Cochran,

> Washington's physician and confidant. . . . I hinted my con-
> fidence that these commotions would not separate us from
> Great Britain; that Washington would one day bring about
> the reunion and be rewarded with an Irish peerage. I have
> no doubt of his repeating it to him [Washington], nor but
> that the idea was flattering to his vanity. His wrath at Arnold
> may be for outrunning him in that race.[28]

William Smith seems to have become Benedict Arnold's

26 *Ibid.*, 8.
27 Van Doren, *Secret History*, 318.
28 *Ibid.*

chief adviser and ghost writer after the General's defection. It
is obvious that Arnold's address "To the Inhabitants of America," printed in *The Royal Gazette,* October 11, 1780, was
written by William Smith, although based on Arnold's notes
and altered before publication by the general. This can be
traced through Smith's *Diary:*

> October 3. A letter this morning from General Arnold re-
> questing a draft of an address from him to the public. I had
> doubts of complying and only promised by a note to assist
> on his draft.
> October 4. I sent General Arnold draft of address to the
> public.
> October 5. He calls, alters the first, and shows new draft of
> the last; copies the former and throws draft into the fire
> with his notes of it. Begins to copy my alterations or addi-
> tions to the intelligence.[29]

Smith also wrote Arnold's "Proclamation to the Officers and
Soldiers of the Continental Army," printed in the *Gazette* on
October 25, 1780.[30]

As an intelligence officer William Smith also took part in the
British attempt to win Vermont for the Crown. This attempt
revolved about Ethan Allen's efforts to have Vermont recognized as a separate government. Congress refused to do this in
deference to New York, which claimed the area. The British
negotiations would have involved recognition of the government of Vermont in return for recognition of the supremacy of
British government in North America.

William Smith apparently had a flair for intelligence work,
for he was able to develop his own spy and courier network
which carried on all negotiations with the Allens after Sir

---

[29] William Smith Mss. Diary, VI, New York Public Library. It was on
October 5, 1780, that news reached New York City of Andre's execution.
Arnold was with Smith working on his address when he heard the news.
According to Smith, Arnold was "vastly disconcerted" at the reports.
[30] Van Doren, *Secret History,* 377.

Henry Clinton's network had been uncovered by Washington's secret service. However, the British negotiations with Vermont failed, at least partially because William Smith had no intention of allowing them to succeed. Successful negotiations between the British and Vermont would have had as a concomitant factor the repudiation of New York's claims to a large part of Vermont. This land had been granted by New York, in the colonial period, to New Yorkers, including William Smith and the Livingston family. As in the MacDougall affair of 1770 Smith carried out a dual role. He betrayed the negotiations he was engaged in to Governor George Clinton and succeeded in stopping them.[31] Although Sir Henry Clinton did not mention this episode in his memoirs, it is obvious that he suspected the Chief Justice, but had no proof. Smith remained under a shadow until Sir Guy Carleton replaced Clinton in New York. At that time Smith returned to official favor.

Andrew Allen's career during the Revolution resembled both Alexander's and Smith's in some respects. After withdrawing from Congress in 1776, Allen went to New York where he swore an oath of allegiance to the king and renounced those he had taken as a member of the Continental Congress. Both he and his brother, William Allen, Jr., were prominent among the Loyalist refugees in New York City. William Allen, Jr. served as colonel in command of the Pennsylvania Loyalists, a militia regiment that served under Howe at Brandywine Creek and in Philadelphia after its capture on September 26, 1777. Previous to that time Howe had named Andrew Allen lieutenant governor of Pennsylvania. Allen served in that capacity, in Philadelphia, until its evacuation in June, 1778 and kept the title until the end of the war. Because he served as an official for the British government of the province, Andrew Allen was attained for high treason by the Commonwealth of Pennsyl-

---

[31] WS Diary (Upton), xxiii. Chilton Williamson, Vermont in Quandary: 1763–1825 (Montpelier, Vermont, 1949), 92–115. A. J. H. Richardson, "Chief Justice William Smith and the Haldimand Negotiation," Proceedings of the Vermont Historical Society, n.s., IX, 1941, 84–114.

vania and his estates, all in Philadelphia, were confiscated.[32] He later estimated that his confiscated estate was worth more than £20,000. In addition Allen, because of his loyalty to the crown, lost his income of over £1,000 *per annum.*[33]

Although he held a position of some authority under the crown, Andrew Allen, like William Smith, was apparently also not fully trusted by the Tories. Even after the war while in exile in England he seems to have encountered hostility. One Tory testifying to Allen's loyalty in 1785 stated that "the great proprietors of Lands thought if they could be Independent of this Country they should be petty princes, but when they saw that the Rebels confiscated their Estates they turn's about & became very loyal. . . . There can not be a more Loyal Man than Mr [Andrew] Allen is *at this Moment.*"[34] It is apparently for this reason that Allen left New York and went to England before the end of the war.

Behaving in Europe as a gentleman of wealth and fashion, Allen spent the "season" at Spa in 1782, where he became instrumental in the defection of Silas Deane to the British. Andrew Allen and Silas Deane had first become acquainted while both were serving in the Continental Congress. They chanced to meet again at Spa in October, 1782. In their conversations there, and later in Brussels, Deane revealed his bitterness at the treatment he had received from Congress and concluded that, in Allen's words, "some Degree of Union with Great Britain was absolutely necessary to the future Peace & Prosperity of America." Allen seized upon this bait and asked Deane if he could communicate these sentiments to the British government. Deane was agreeable, provided that "such Intercourse could be arranged with Secresy." His usefulness would be at an end if it were known that he was in communication with the British government, but "he would cheerfully confer

---

32 *The Claim and Answer . . . in the case of Andrew Allen against the United States, Under the [Jay] Treaty* (Philadelphia, 1799), 8.

33 American Loyaltists, Commission of Enquiry, III, 400.

34 *Ibid.,* 401. Italics mine.

with any confidential Person sent over by Government to the Continent."[35] Andrew Allen thereby became Deane's first link with the British and seems to have served the Earl of Shelburne in some confidential capacity during the closing years of the war.

When the peace treaty ending the American Revolution was signed in September, 1783, the Tories were faced with the problem of establishing new homes and careers. Our Whig-Loyalists, with the exception of Daniel Dulany and William Samuel Johnson, faced the same difficulties. Three of them remained in relative obscurity for the remainder of their lives, but the other four made a remarkable recovery and achieved a rebirth of political prominence either in the British Empire or, surprisingly, in the independent United States. There seems to have been a remarkable absence of bitterness towards the United States among the Whig-Loyalists which enabled them to resettle either there or elsewhere without hostility towards the new nation.

Andrew Allen, Robert Alexander and Daniel Dulany were among those who remained in obscurity after the Revolution. Robert Alexander, having been outlawed by Maryland, left New York City towards the end of 1783 and arrived in England in January, 1784. The Loyalist Claims Commission awarded him £5,450 and an annual pension of £220 for his services and losses in the British cause. He returned to the practice of law, but was probably not happy during his stay in London for he never again saw his family, who remained in Maryland.[36] He died in London on November 20, 1805.

Andrew Allen also lived out his life in England in relative obscurity. However, he visited Pennsylvania in 1792 after being pardoned by the state. With the ratification of the Jay Treaty, Allen attempted to recover the money paid to Pennsylvania

[35] Andrew Allen to the Earl of Shelburne, October 17, 1782; Shelburne Papers, University of Michigan.
[36] Johnson, *Robert Alexander,* 123.

for his confiscated lands, but failed to receive any satisfaction from the American courts. It is probable that he practiced law in London. He received a £400 pension from the Crown until his death on March 7, 1825.[37]

Daniel Dulany remained in Maryland, but never returned to political office after the Revolution. He did practice law as an expert consultant, but does not seem to have been consulted at all by the leaders of the new national or state governments.[38] However his life was a happy one until his death and his family was reunited for a time when his son Dan returned from England in 1785. Daniel Dulany III seems to have been a friend of George Washington's, for he rode to Washington's hounds in Virginia and partook of upper class Chesapeake society during his stay in the United States. He later returned to England as a British citizen.[39] Daniel Dulany, the subject of our sketch, died in Maryland on March 17, 1797.

Daniel Leonard and William Smith both achieved very high positions in the British empire. Their rise is all the more remarkable when one considers that even such prominent Tories as Joseph Galloway, William Franklin and Peter Oliver, all of whom received large pensions, were never appointed to prominent positions by the British government. Daniel Leonard spent the war years in London and in 1782 was appointed Chief Justice of Bermuda. He held the position until 1806 and, as he was stationed in the western hemisphere, visited Massachusetts several times to care for family and business matters. But he had no intention of ever settling in his old home again. Yet, as with all exiles, ties to his home remained and, in 1826, Leonard was considering a return to Massachusetts, so "that I may lie by the side of my Father."[40] When he returned to London in 1806 he practiced law and for many

---

37 Keith, "Andrew Allen," 364.

38 Land, *Dulanys of Maryland*, 332–333.

39 *Ibid.*, 330–331.

40 Daniel Leonard to Judge Laban Wheaton, July 23, 1826; Daniel Leonard Papers, Old Colony Historical Society, Taunton, Massachusetts.

years was considered to be the dean of English barristers. At the age of ninety he died as the result of a self inflicted accidental pistol wound on June 27, 1829.[41]

As has been noted, Chief Justice William Smith had never been fully trusted by the Tories of New York. This was partly because Smith continually placed the blame for the American Revolution "to the pride & avarice of Great Britain, in assuming an authority, inconsistent with the compact by which the empire had long been prosperously united."[42] When the war ended he did not want to leave America for exile in England and made efforts to remain. In August, 1783 Smith wrote to William Samuel Johnson regarding his chances of obtaining a place of refuge in Connecticut.[43] Johnson offered no encouragement and Smith decided to leave America.[44] He sailed for England in 1783 as a member of Sir Guy Carleton's staff. In 1786 Carleton, now Baron Dorchester, was named Governor of Quebec. Through his influence William Smith was appointed Chief Justice of that province. During the postwar years Smith never gave up his ideas of empire or the hope of reuniting the United States with the British empire. For this reason he never returned to New York although an act of the New York Assembly permitted William Smith and seven other Loyalists to return to the state without jeopardy. He died at Quebec on December 3, 1793.

Although William Samuel Johnson discouraged William Smith from seeking refuge in Connecticut after the Revolution, Johnson himself was still influential in Connecticut politics despite his loyalty to England through most of the war years. His career after the Revolution was without parallel

---

[41] Obituary notice, *Bermuda Royal Gazette*, August 25, 1829.

[42] William Smith, *The Candid Retrospect: or, The American War Examined, by Whig Principles* (Charleston, South Carolina, 1780; New York, 1781.)

[43] William Smith to William Samuel Johnson, August 23, 1783; William Samuel Johnson Papers, Connecticut Historical Society.

[44] William Samuel Johnson to William Smith, October 25, 1783; William Smith Papers, New York Public Library.

among Loyalists and constitutes a unique chapter in the history of American Loyalism. Johnson had lost a great deal of his political power and influence during the war, but quickly regained his place in the Connecticut oligarchy after the signing of the peace treaty. In 1784 the Connecticut Assembly appointed William Samuel Johnson to a seat in Congress. He took office on January 13, 1785. At the spring elections in Connecticut he was popularly elected to Congress and was returned to a seat on the Council by the second largest vote in the state. In 1787 he was reelected to both positions.[45]

Having regained a position of leadership in the state, Johnson proceeded to win success as a national statesman in the Federal Constitutional Convention. Before the writing of the Constitution the populace of Connecticut was strongly anti-federal in sentiment, but substantial federalist feelings were manifested by most Connecticut newspapers. Noah Webster of the *Connecticut Courant* (Hartford) and Josiah Meigs of the *New-Haven Gazette* were extremely influential members of this group.[46] Johnson's Congressional colleague, Stephen Mix Mitchell, was an active Federalist, but Johnson believed that the chances of success for the Federal Convention were "very problematical."[47] Yet in May, 1787 William Samuel Johnson was elected a Connecticut delegate to the convention. It was at Philadelphia that Johnson emerged as a national statesman. He was an advocate of compromise and succeeded in conciliating "small state" men and "big state" men. Johnson was also able to help secure the adoption of a two-house legislature. In addition, he supported Hamilton's plan for the assumption of state debts. It is questionable whether this was because he was a speculator in securities, dealing through his son Robert Charles Johnson, as Charles Beard has sug-

---

[45] Groce, *William Samuel Johnson,* 118–119, 127.

[46] B. C. Steiner, "Connecticut's Ratification of the Federal Constitution," American Antiquarian Society *Proceedings,* XXV, 1915, 70–80.

[47] Groce, *William Samuel Johnson,* 137.

gested.[48] Although Johnson signed the Constitution at Philadelphia, he was not active in securing its adoption in Connecticut. Despite this inactivity he was elected to the Connecticut Ratifying Convention where he stated his fears that if the Constitution was not adopted "our national existence must come to a final end."[49]

On the same day as he was elected to the Ratifying Convention, William Samuel Johnson accepted the presidency of Columbia College in New York. This appointment was very congenial to Dr. Johnson, for his father had served in the same capacity before the Revolution.[50] He no longer resided in Connecticut, but the Assembly of that state appointed him to a six-year term as first United States Senator from Connecticut. He accepted the appointment because, with the capital located in New York City, he could serve as president of Columbia and Senator at the same time. Johnson, due to his activities at Columbia, was not as active in the Senate as he had been in Congress, but showed himself to be a moderate Federalist. Besides supporting Hamilton's plan for the assumption of state debts, he voted for the establishment of the Bank of the United States and became a shareholder in it. Johnson also helped to draft the Judiciary Act of 1791, supported the maintenance of a standing army, and worked for the admission of Kentucky and Vermont to the union. But he found himself in opposition to the Federalists when he voted against allowing the President to remove his appointments from office without the consent of the Senate.

When the capital was moved to Philadelphia William Sam-

---

[48] Charles A. Beard, *An Economic Interpretation of the Constitution of the United States* (New York, 1913; 2nd. edn., New York, 1935), 117–118. For an account of Johnson's role in the Convention see: Groce, *William Samuel Johnson*, 139–151.

[49] Address of January 4, 1788; Groce, *William Samuel Johnson*, 156.

[50] William Samuel Johnson became first president of Columbia College. His father had been first president of Columbia's predecessor, King's College.

uel Johnson was forced to choose between the Senate and
Columbia College. He decided to remain in the academic
world and resigned from the Senate in March, 1791 after
serving two years of his six-year term. He then served Columbia in several capacities besides that of president. At times
he taught logic, belles lettres, and rhetoric. In 1800 however
he was forced to resign as president because of serious illness.
Johnson suffered from gout, a palsied hand and deafness.
Because of his infirmities he never again held public office and
wrote no letters after 1803. He was an invalid until his death
on November 14, 1819, closed one of the most remarkable
careers of the eighteenth century.

Daniel Leonard had lived in London during the war and
it seems found the city an agreeable place to reside. But many
Loyalists did not enjoy their sojourns in England. Among
them was the Whig-Loyalist Peter Van Schaack. Van Schaack
changed his opinion of England after observations of the
country at first hand. He began to believe that the British
government wanted only "to draw from the Colonies a substantial, solid revenue" and make the crown more influential
in colonial affairs. Van Schaack felt that corruption, dissipa-
tion, depravity and luxury had become the dominant features
of the British system of government. From these observations
he found his "mind totally absolved from all ideas of duty."
He saw "the British constitution in its most essential principles
totally lost." As a firm believer in Locke's principles he believed himself to be absolved from his allegiance to the crown
and that he had therefore reverted to a state of nature and
become "a citizen of the world." He therefore determined to
return to his native land.[51] Van Schaack wrote to John Jay
regarding his chances of being able to return to New York.
He stated that he considered himself to be "a citizen of the
United States, *de jure* at least, whether [he] became so *de*

---

[51] Diary, 1780; Van Schaack, *Peter Van Schaack*, 263.

facto or not."[52] Jay, upon his return to the United States after the signing of the peace treaty, worked to get the act of attainder against Van Schaack reversed.[53] This accomplished, Peter Van Schaack landed in New York in July, 1785.

Upon his return Van Schaack discovered that his estates had never been confiscated and a few months after his return to Kinderhook an act of the legislature restored him to citizenship. He was readmitted to the bar and opened a law office in his native town. Soon thereafter Peter Van Schaack returned to active political life. When the Constitution was presented to New York State for ratification, Van Schaack was nominated as the Federalist candidate to the ratifying convention from Columbia County where Kinderhook was located. However the county was strongly anti-federalist and he lost the election "without being much mortified. The popular tide was against us, that is (to be sure) against what was *right* and *good*."[54] Although he was offered a Federalist nomination to run for Congress, Van Schaack refused. He had determined, because of his poor eyesight, that upon his return from exile he would keep out of public life. His actions at the time of ratification were "an exception to the rule, not an infraction of it. It was a peculiar case and justified by the *occasion*."[55]

Peter Van Schaack believed that he could do more for the good of America as a private citizen than as a government official. His strong convictions about the law led him to question the prevailing apprenticeship method of training lawyers. This he believed did not produce good lawyers as a rule, but afforded established attorneys the opportunity of obtaining clerical help at a low salary. He therefore opened a law school

[52] Peter Van Schaack to John Jay, August 5, 1783; *ibid.*, 309.

[53] John Jay to Peter Van Schaack, September 8, 1784; John Jay Collection, Columbia University Library.

[54] Peter Van Schaack to Henry Walton, June 3, 1788; Van Schaack, *Peter Van Schaack*, 425.

[55] Peter Van Schaack to Henry Van Schaack, February 22, 1789; *ibid.*, 429–430.

in his home. It provided legal training in various subjects and is considered by the legal historian Paul Hamlin to be the first law school in America.[56] Although he was almost blind, Van Schaack continued to practice law until 1812 and had students until 1826. He was considered to be a fine teacher and in forty years trained almost 100 young lawyers. Many prominent jurists, including Rufus King and Theodore Sedgwick, sent their sons to study under him. Because of his services to the bar, Columbia University conferred a Doctor of Laws degree on Peter Van Schaack in 1826. He died at Kinderhook on September 27, 1832.

The years immediately following the war were difficult ones for the Loyalists. Throughout the Revolution they had been fighting to preserve the America into which they had been born and raised; or, like William Smith, to establish the colonies as an integral but co-equal partner in the British empire. With the establishment of American independence, the Loyalists lost not only their homes, but their cause as well. They were faced with the problem of building new homes and careers for themselves in an alien land—be it England, Canada or the West Indies. Most prominent Loyalists never achieved positions of preeminence among the British; thus the Whig-Loyalists stand as a group apart. Unlike many of the Tories, the Whig-Loyalists were not bitter about the outcome of the American Revolution. In many respects this may be attributed to the fact that in character and political thought they were essentially Whigs and, before 1776, Patriots. Because of this they were more resilient than most Tories. The Whig-Loyalists found it easier to rebound from the loss of their homes. Two of the Whig-Loyalists, William Smith and Daniel Leonard, became chief justices of royal colonies. Leonard, Andrew Allen and Robert Alexander practiced law successfully in London, although the clientele of the latter

[56] Paul Mahlon Hamlin, *Legal Education in Colonial New York* (New York, 1939), 69.

two seem to have been made up primarily of other displaced Americans. Of perhaps more significance is the fact that three of the Whig-Loyalists were able to reestablish themselves in the United States. Daniel Dulany did not regain the eminent position in Maryland politics that he had occupied before the Revolution but was still highly thought of as a lawyer. Peter Van Schaack was also recognized as a fine attorney and, although he did not play an active role in the politics of the new nation, was offered a Federalist nomination to Congress. William Samuel Johnson was able to reestablish his position to such an extent that he became first United States Senator from Connecticut and first president of Columbia College.

The Whig-Loyalists were thus unique among the Loyalists even after the war. Explanations of the phenomenon known as Whig-Loyalism must necessarily be conjectural in some respects. There was no personal link among all nine of the men under discussion. To be sure, some of them knew each other. The professional class in colonial America was small; its members knew each other, at least by reputation. And so, Dr. Benjamin Church and Daniel Leonard were acquainted; William Smith and William Samuel Johnson were friends; Peter Van Schaack was Smith's student. Daniel Dulany and Robert Alexander were undoubtedly known to one another; William Byrd III was probably acquainted with Daniel Dulany; Robert Alexander and Andrew Allen met as members of Congress. But these nine men by no means constituted a clique. Yet all of them were very similar in some ways and espoused a political ideology, in accordance with which, they functioned in much the same fashion during the revolutionary era.

Unlike the Tories, the Whig-Loyalists were part of the mainstream of American political thought in the years before the Declaration of Independence. William Smith and Peter Van Schaack in particular considered themselves to be Lockean philosophers. In all cases they were members of the colonial Whig oligarchies, most of whose members were Patriots. For this reason the Whig-Loyalists cannot be identified with the Tories. Their reasons for supporting the British cause after July 4, 1776, were dissimilar. The Whig-Loyalists supported the crown because of a concept of empire and a political philosophy which was essentially Lockean. They considered themselves to be Americans or British Americans, unlike many of the Tories who believed that they were Englishmen who happened to have been born in the colonies. The Whig-Loyalists differed with the Patriots only over the necessity of independence, believing it possible to be co-equal partners with the English in the British empire. This undoubtedly helps to explain why some of them regained political eminence after the Revolution. They were fundamentally activists, taking a prominent part in the pre-revolutionary conflict. Much of the course of the revolutionary struggle had been guided by the Whig-Loyalists and they did not object to the general trend taken by the conflict. They objected only to the concept of independence. While the Tories were upset by the whole impact of the 1765–1783 struggle, the Whig-Loyalists could and did feel that much of this was their handiwork. Hence, they could not be as corrosively bitter about American independence as Tories like Thomas Hutchinson, Peter Oliver or Joseph Galloway.

The Whig-Loyalists were not unique among Whigs in their hesitancy over the question of independence. Many Patriots—notably John Dickinson, John Jay, Robert R. Livingston and Robert Morris—believed the measure to be too radical in 1776 and were slow in supporting the move. Thus many men in the mainstream of American political thought during the 1760's and 1770's hesitated when the Declaration of Independence was promulgated; the Whig-Loyalists rejected it, others acquiesced.

The American Tories were profoundly alienated from American society in the years before the Revolution. When the war ended in American victory, the Tories lost not only their homes, but their identity as well. In England they were forced to make a fundamental adjustment. They were not Englishmen; at least they were not treated as Englishmen by those born in England. It is true that the Whig-Loyalists who remained in England were also confronted with the problem of being aliens in a foreign land. But they had not expected to feel immediately at home in England and thus were able to respond to the English scene much more rapidly than were the Tories who had an additional mental adjustment to undergo. Several of the Whig-Loyalists were also able to regain political prominence in the United States, an achievement the Tories never considered. Because their political philosophy was similar in essence to that of the Patriots, because they had been part of the Whig ruling structure before the Revolution, and because they had ties of friendship and family with the new leadership, the Whig-Loyalists were able to regain their prominence with relative ease.

The existence of a political philosophy such as Whig-Loyalism demonstrates the depth and strength of American attachment to the British empire. The Loyalist cause, as of 1776, consisted not merely of the long beleaguered Tories who were isolated, hardened and embittered by a decade of abuse from patriotic agitators, but also of important last minute Whig recruits, men of ability and vigor who had helped to shape the revolutionary cause. These men, motivated by affection for the empire and by fear of social upheaval, could not accept Thomas Jefferson's call to dissolve the long established political bands that tied the empire together and rejected the concept of independence.

BIBLIOGRAPHICAL ESSAY

This essay makes no pretense of being comprehensive or definitive. It is hoped that it will be useful for those interested in proceeding further in the study of revolutionary political ideology in general and Whig-Loyalism in particular.

Any study of revolutionary political ideology must begin with Bernard Bailyn, *The Ideological Origins of the American Revolution* (Cambridge, Massachusetts, 1967) which is a development of the General Introduction to the first volume of *Pamphlets of the American Revolution* (Cambridge, Massachusetts, 1965). Professor Bailyn has presented us with the most enlightening interpretation of revolutionary ideology yet to appear in print. He considers 1776 to have been an intellectual revolution in the sense that it marked a transformation of the American mind that led to the emergence of ideas and attitudes incompatible with society as it existed in pre-revolutionary America. Bailyn links the attitudes of the American revolutionaries with the anti-authoritarian tradition of Caroline Robbins's seventeenth century English "commonwealthmen," demonstrating their influence in colonial America. To Bailyn, the American Revolution was "an ideological-constitutional struggle and not primarily a controversy between social groups undertaken to force changes in the organization of society." The author is in complete agreement with this statement.

In attempting to form a comprehension of the ideology of revolutionary leaders an invaluable study has been written by H. Trevor Colbourn, *The Lamp of Experience: Whig History and the Intellectual Origins of the American Revolution* (Chapel Hill, 1965). Professor Colbourn analyses the historical learning of the leading Patriots, which, with the study of law, was their prime literary concern. The Patriots viewed their struggle against the arbitrary power of Great Britain in an historical perspective colored by the prevailing notions of a Whig interpretation of history. This Whig interpretation stressed the myth of a Saxon democracy without feudal land tenure, an established church or a standing army.[1] It provided for an elective monarchy and annual Parliaments, and Americans tended to write, as William Smith did, of a "grand Wittenagemott." The Patriots stressed the tyranny of the Norman Conquest and the uphill struggle to restore Saxon freedom of which their revolution was the culmination. There is no doubt that the ideology of the American Revolution is inexplicable without an understanding of the Whig historical perspective of the leaders of that struggle.

Robert R. Palmer, *The Age of the Democratic Revolution* (2 vols., Princeton, 1959–1964) and Jack P. Greene, *The Quest for Power: The Lower Houses of Assembly in the Southern Royal Colonies 1689–1776* (Chapel Hill, 1963) provide fine expositions of the role of oligarchy in the developing American struggle. Palmer shows how the colonial oligarchies, from which most of the revolutionary leaders emerged, were based on far more democratic institutions than those of Great Britain. Greene documents the development of lower house power and capacity for leadership. He shows how they responded to new imperial policies as a challenge to their own oligarchic power. To Professor Greene, the central issue of the Revolution was the attempt by the assemblies to preserve their own powers.

The best available work on loyalism is William H. Nelson, *The American Tory* (Oxford, 1961). This brief volume provides a useful survey of the general problem, although I disagree with Dr. Nelson on several matters of interpretation. The breadth and depth of his research are disappointing. He confined his attention to generally available printed sources and ignored several major documents such as the notes of *The Royal Commission on the Losses and Services of Ameri-*

---

[1] On the influence of standing armies in revolutionary America see: William A. Benton, "Pennsylvania Revolutionary Officers and the Federal Constitution," *Pennsylvania History*, XXXI, 1964.

can Loyalists (available on microfilm at the New York Public Library). However, Nelson's book is well written and more penetrating than Claude H. Van Tyne, *The Loyalists in the American Revolution* (New York, 1902).

Lawrence Henry Gipson, *The British Empire Before the American Revolution* (13 vols. to date, Caldwell, Idaho and New York, 1936–1967) provides the finest survey of the pre-revolutionary period in print. The breadth, clarity and penetration of Professor Gipson's research is without parallel among contemporary historians.

Any discussion of the colonial response to the Stamp Act must take Edmund S. and Helen M. Morgan's excellent study *The Stamp Act Crisis: Prologue to Revolution* (Chapel Hill, 1953) into account. Their thesis is that a devotion to principle was the animating factor for colonial resistance to the Stamp Act. They argue that this controversy crystallized revolutionary and counter-revolutionary attitudes in America. The Morgans conclude that although "the situation was not irretrievable" at the time of the repeal of the Stamp Act, "there was nevertheless a genuine and irreconcilable conflict between Parliament's insistence on its authority to tax the colonies and the American's denial of that authority." Edmund S. Morgan has also edited a book of documents, *Prologue to Revolution: Sources and Documents on the Stamp Act Crisis, 1764–1766* (Chapel Hill, 1959). Although designed for student use, it is the finest and most complete collection of documents on the period.

The starting point for a study of the bishopric controversy is Arthur Lyon Cross, *The Anglican Episcopate and the American Colonies* (1902; reprinted: Hamden, Connecticut, 1964). Carl Bridenbaugh's brilliant study *Mitre and Sceptre: Transatlantic Faiths, Ideas, Personalities, and Politics* (New York, 1962) was intended by its author to "supplement rather than to replace" Cross's study and "to deal with matters he did not investigate." Professor Bridenbaugh did just that, using newly available materials and making new appraisals. His very convincing thesis concerning the bishopric controversy is that the Church of England should share responsibility for the American Revolution along with the crown and Parliament. Eben

Edwards Beardsley, *The History of the Episcopal Church in Connecticut* (New York, 1868) is useful primarily for William Samuel Johnson's role in the controversy. Alan Heimert, *Religion and the American Mind from the Great Awakening to the Revolution* (Cambridge, Massachusetts, 1966) is a revisionist interpretation of American religious thought as it developed during and after the Great Awakening. According to the author, two religious parties emerged, one opponents (Liberals), the other (Calvinists) advocates of revival. By 1776 the Calvinist position had become an ideology with strong revolutionary, democratic and nationalistic overtones; the Liberal position, an ideology of political conservatism and social elitism. Dr. Heimert considers the episcopacy issue to have been "something of a red herring." This is a weak argument; that espoused by Cross and Bridenbaugh is more convincing.

A study of political leaders in the revolutionary period must, of course, take into account the pertinent literature for each colony being studied. The following books, among others, have been found useful in this regard. For Connecticut, the most authoritative study of the revolutionary period is Oscar Zeichner, *Connecticut's Years of Controversy 1750–1776* (Chapel Hill, 1949). Charles Albro Barker, *The Background of the Revolution in Maryland* (New Haven, 1940) is the best extant study of Maryland in this period; also useful is John Thomas Scharf, *The Chronicles of Baltimore* (Baltimore, 1874). The best available account of Massachusetts during the period is James Truslow Adams, *Revolutionary New England* (Boston, 1923). Also useful, although I do not find his interpretation convincing, is Robert E. Brown, *Middle Class Democracy and the Revolution in Massachusetts, 1691–1780* (Ithaca, New York, 1955). Considering the author's Tory perspective, Thomas Hutchinson's *The History of the Colony and Province of Massachusetts-Bay* (Ed. Lawrence Shaw Mayo; 3 vols., Cambridge, Massachusetts, 1936) is remarkably unbiased and informative.

For New York the best works include Carl Lotus Becker's seminal study, *The History of Political Parties in the Province of New York* (Madison, Wisconsin, 1909; reprinted, 1960);

Wilbur C. Abbott, *New York in the American Revolution* (New York and London, 1929); and Thomas Jefferson Wertenbaker, *Father Knickerbocker Rebels, New York City During the Revolution* (New York, 1948). Theodore Thayer, *Pennsylvania Politics and the Growth of Democracy 1740–1766* (Harrisburg, Pennsylvania, 1953) is the best inquiry into that crucial state. A fine study of the capital of the Commonwealth is found in Carl and Jessica Bridenbaugh, *Rebels and Gentlemen: Philadelphia in the Age of Franklin* (1942; paperback reprint: New York, 1962). The most complete work concerning revolutionary Virginia is Charles S. Sydnor, *Gentlemen Freeholders* (Chapel Hill, 1952). Also very helpful are two books by Carl Bridenbaugh—*Myths and Realities: Societies of the Colonial South* (1952; paperback reprint: New York, 1963) and *Seat of Empire: The Political Role of Eighteenth-Century Williamsburg* (1950; paperback reprint: Charlottesville, Virginia, 1963).

Aside from primary source materials, both printed and manuscript, little has been written about any of the Whig-Loyalists. Only one biography of Robert Alexander has been published: Janet Bassett Johnson, *Robert Alexander, Maryland Loyalist* (New York, 1942). This is a factual, but unsatisfying and non-interpretive study. Some of Alexander's letters have been published in the *Archives of Maryland*. Letters to, from and about Alexander may also be found in the manuscript collections of the Maryland Historical Society and the New York Historical Society.

A brief sketch of the life of Andrew Allen has been written by Charles P. Keith and was published in the *Pennsylvania Magazine of History and Biography*, X (1886). Also useful in examining the Allen family is Ruth Moser Kistler, "William Allen, Pennsylvania Loyalist," *Lehigh County Historical Society Proceedings* (1932). Andrew Allen's political career is documented in the *Minutes of the Provincial Council of Pennsylvania* (15 vols., Harrisburg, 1852). Letters by and about Allen can be found in the Historical Society of Pennsylvania and in the William L. Clements Library, University of Michigan.

No biography has been written about William Byrd III and

information about him must be gleaned from more general works. A few surviving letters can be found in the Virginia Historical Society and the Huntington Library.

As with William Byrd, there is no biography of Dr. Benjamin Church, although Allen French, *General Gage's Informers* (Ann Arbor, 1932) presents the details of Church's treason succinctly and objectively, with a wealth of detail. Many of Dr. Church's political tracts have been printed. His polemic on the Stamp Act, *Liberty and Property Vindicated and the St——pm–n Burnt* (Boston, 1765) has been reprinted in Bailyn (ed.), *Pamphlets of the American Revolution. The Times A Poem* [Boston, 1765] and *An Address of A Provincial Bashaw . . . . By a Son of Liberty* ([Boston], 1769) are available only in their original editions or on microcard. Church's speeches commemorating the Boston Massacre are in Alden T. Vaughan (ed.), *Chronicles of the American Revolution* (New York, 1965).

An excellent biography of Daniel Dulany has been written by Aubrey C. Land, *The Dulanys of Maryland* (Baltimore, 1955). Dulany's Stamp Act pamphlet has been reprinted in Bailyn (ed.), *Pamphlets of the American Revolution,* and many of his letters have been printed in the *Archives of Maryland.* His "Antilon" letters have been compiled in Elihu Samuel Riley (ed.), *Correspondence of "First Citizen"–Charles Carroll of Carrollton, and "Antilon"–Daniel Dulany, Jr.* (Baltimore, 1902). Dulany's manuscript letters can be found in the Maryland Historical Society, Harvard College Library and the William L. Clements Library.

Two biographies exist for William Samuel Johnson: Eben Edwards Beardsley, *Life and Times of William Samuel Johnson* (New York, 1876) and George Cuthbert Groce, Jr., *William Samuel Johnson: A Maker of the Constitution* (New York, 1937). Both are factual, but the Groce biography is more interpretive and readable. Johnson's political philosophy has been summarized in Evarts Boutell Greene, "William Samuel Johnson and the American Revolution," *Columbia University Quarterly,* XXII (1930). Letters to and from William Samuel Johnson may be found in *The Trumbull Papers, Collections* of the Massachusetts Historical Society, 5th series, IX (Boston,

1885) and in the *Papers* of the New Haven Colony Historical Society, IX (1918). In addition, manuscript correspondence can be found in the Columbia University Library, Connecticut Historical Society, Harvard College Library, and the New York Public Library.

A study of the life of Daniel Leonard is available in Ralph Davol, *Two Men of Taunton* (Taunton, Massachusetts, 1912). This is a dual biography of Daniel Leonard and Robert Treat Paine. Paine, as a signer of the Declaration of Independence, is a hero to the author; therefore, the treatment of Leonard is fairly cursory. Leonard's "Massachusettensis" letters have been collected in *Novanglus and Massachusettensis* (Boston, 1819). Leonard's letters are found in the Massachusetts Historical Society and in the Old Colony Historical Society, Taunton, Massachusetts.

While no biography of William Smith, Jr. has been published, a great deal of information is available in print about his life. The introductions to *The Diary and Selected Papers of Chief Justice William Smith 1784–1793* (Ed. L.F.S. Upton; Toronto, 1963) and *Historical Memoirs* (Ed. William H. W. Sabine; 2 vols., New York, 1956–1958) are both well written and informative. Dorothy Rita Dillon, *The New York Triumvirate* (New York, 1949) is a good study of the political careers of William Smith, William Livingston, and John Morin Scott, but it does not answer the critical question of why these men took three different ideological courses during the revolutionary era. Smith's services as a Loyalist are described in Carl Van Doren, *Secret History of the American Revolution* (New York, 1941), Chilton Williamson, *Vermont in Quandary: 1763–1825* (Montpelier, Vermont, 1949) and A. J. H. Richardson, "Chief Justice William Smith and the Haldimand Negotiation," *Proceedings* of the Vermont Historical Society, n.s., IX (1941). His post-war career is detailed in Hilda M. Neatby, "Chief Justice William Smith: an 18th Century Whig Imperialist," *Canadian Historical Review*, XXVIII (1947). Tory views of William Smith may be found in Thomas Jones, *History of New York During the Revolutionary War* (Ed. Edward F. DeLancey; 2 vols., New York, 1879) and Cadwallader

Colden's writings printed in the *Collections* of the New York Historical Society.

Many of William Smith's political writings are available in modern editions, including *The Independent Reflector* (Ed. Milton M. Klein; Cambridge, Massachusetts, 1963); "Observations on America" (Ed. Oscar Zeichner), *New York History*, XXIII (1942); and "Thoughts upon the Dispute between Great Britain and her Colonies," in Robert M. Calhoon, "William Smith, Jr's. Alternative to the American Revolution," *William and Mary Quarterly*, 3rd series, XXII (1965). His valuable *The History of the Late Province of New-York* (2 vols., New York, 1829) should be reprinted. Unpublished writings and letters of William Smith can be found in the New York Public Library.

Henry Cruger Van Schaack, *The Life of Peter Van Schaack* (New York, 1842) is not really a biography, but is an invaluable collection of letters and diary extracts, many of which are not available elsewhere. In addition, Peter Van Schaack's correspondence may be found in the Columbia University Library and in the New York Historical Society.

INDEX

Adair, Robert, opposes Stamp Act, 63

Adams, John, 13, 38, 102, 189; opposition to Stamp Act, 14, 79; opinion of William Smith, William Livingston and John M. Scott, 24, 154; friend of Daniel Leonard, 37; friend of Benjamin Church, 39; on smuggled tea, 101; opposes establishment of American bishopric, 107, 119; on Boston Tea Party, 124; on Daniel Leonard, 125–126, 128; on Benjamin Church, 143–144

Adams, Samuel, 13, 39, 40, 125

Alexander, Robert, 13, 21, 33, 40, 82, 120, 154; early life, 34–35; opposes Stamp Act, 63, 79; opposes Townshend Acts, 91–92, 100; opposes Coercive Acts, 131–132; supports Continental Association, 138–139; elected to Maryland Convention, 140; on war with England, 145–146; elected to Second Continental Congress, 147–150, 153–154; advocates independence, 150; on Declaration of Independence, 161, 163–165, 171; becomes a Loyalist, 164–165; during war years, 190, 195–197; attempts to return to Maryland, 195–196;

outlawed for high treason, 196; Director of Associated Loyalists, 196–197; lives in England after the Revolution, 203, 210

Alexander, William, father of Robert Alexander, 34–35

Alison, Francis, opposes establishment of American bishopric, 107–108

Allen, Andrew, 13, 21, 35, 40, 87, 120, 154; early life, 31–33; opposes Stamp Act, 76, 79; on repeal of Townshend Acts, 100; member of Council of Safety, 146–147; elected to Second Continental Congress, 147–150, 153; on Declaration of Independence, 161–162, 163, 171; during war years, 190, 201–203; lieutenant governor of Pennsylvania, 201; attainted for high treason, 201–202; instrumental in defection of Silas Deane, 202–203; lives in England after the Revolution, 203–204, 210

Allen, Ethan, 199–200

Allen, James, brother of Andrew Allen, 31–32; opposes Stamp Act, 76

Allen, John, brother of Andrew Allen, 76; opposes Stamp Act, 76; becomes a Loyalist, 162

223

224

DATE DUE

MAR 26 '73			
APR 12 '73			
APR 11 '74			